CW00694298

Berlitz

VENICE
POCKET GUIDE

Walking Eye
mobile app

Discover the world's best destinations with the Insight Guides Walking Eye app, available to download for free in the App Store and Google Play.

The container app provides easy access to fantastic free content on events and activities taking place in your current location or chosen destination, with the possibility of booking, as well as the regularly-updated Insight Guides travel blog: Inspire Me. In addition, you can purchase curated, premium destination guides through the app, which feature local highlights, hotel, bar, restaurant and shopping listings, an A to Z of practical information and more. Or purchase and download Insight Guides eBooks straight to your device.

TOP 10 ATTRACTIONS

THE RIALTO
The historic heart of Venice's commercial quarter is still famed for its markets. See page 62.

PALAZZO DUCALE
The splendid former home of the Venetian doges. See page 35.

COLLEZIONE PEGGY GUGGENHEIM
One of the best modern art collections in Europe. See page 54.

SCUOLA GRANDE DI SAN ROCCO
The interior is decorated with many of Tintoretto's finest paintings. See page 66.

MURANO

This island is world-renowned for the fine glass that has been made here for centuries. See page 80.

BASILICA DI SAN MARCO

The magnificent church at the very heart of Venice. See page 27.

BRIDGE OF SIGHS

Links the Palazzo Ducale with the former jail. See page 38.

THE ACCADEMIA

Home to the magnificent pre-eminent collection of Venetian art from the 14th to 18th centuries. See page 50.

LA SALUTE

This iconic landmark stands at the entrance to the Grand Canal. See page 55.

THE GRAND CANAL

The city's spectacular main artery is lined with old palaces. See page 73.

A PERFECT DAY

9.00am

Morning market
Feast your eyes on the fish, fruit and vegetables of the Rialto markets, where stalls have been in business for over 1,000 years. Watch the barges offloading at the quayside, then browse in local delis for spices, coffee and cheeses.

1.00pm

Lunch with a view
Take your pick from the open-air cafés and restaurants on the Zattere, the panoramic quayside skirting the southern side of the Dorsoduro. For dessert try Gelateria Nico, one of the best ice cream parlours in town.

11.00am

Gallery visit
You're now in the *sestiere* of Dorsoduro, a haven for art lovers, home to the Accademia and Guggenheim galleries. Explore the Accademia, housing the world's greatest collection of Venetian art, before watching the mesmerising water traffic on the Accademia Bridge.

2.00pm

Gentle stroll
Stretch your legs along the Zattere, popping into the Gesuati church to check out the Tiepolo ceiling. Head to the tip of the peninsula where the Punta della Dogana has been transformed into a cutting-edge contemporary art gallery, then go admire the monumental La Salute basilica.

10.00am

Grand Canal
From the Rialto take *vaporetto* No. 1 in the San Marco/Lido direction. Glide past the parade of palaces and alight at Accademia.

IN VENICE

4.00pm

San Marco tea

Splash out on tea at Caffè Florian in Piazza San Marco, then wander along the Riva degli Schiavoni quayside, taking in the views across to the island of San Giorgio Maggiore.

6.30pm

Quiet drink

Leave the crowds behind and explore the streets and squares of the Castello region behind the Riva. Join the locals in a bar for an *ombrà* (glass of wine), Prosecco or *spritz* (a Venetian aperitif), accompanied by *cichetti*, tapas-like snacks.

10.00pm

Last drink

Cross the Giudecca canal by *vaporetto* to Skyline, a cool rooftop haunt in the Hilton Molino Stucky, suspended over the lagoon. With its superb views and stylish cocktails, Skyline is the best way to end your day in Venice.

3.00pm

Bellini time

Hop on a *vaporetto* to Vallaresso landing stage across the Grand Canal. Pass Harry's Bar (popping in for a bellini if you can't resist) and head north to Salizzada San Moisé and Calle Larga XXII Marzo to browse some of the smartest shops in town.

8.00pm

Romantic dinner on the Zattere

Enjoy a romantic dinner in Lineadombra (Dorsoduro 19, Fondamenta Zattere Ai Saloni, tel: 041-241 1881) a simple, elegant design-conscious restaurant that is challenging Venetian stereotypes.

CONTENTS

INTRODUCTION

Venice is the place we have all been to, if only in our imagination. For an unbroken 1,100 years *La Serenissima*, the Serene Republic was an independent empire, with a constitution that is studied to this day. In the 9th century, while most European cities were hidden behind defensive walls, Venice stood open to the world, protected only by its lagoon. As a tantalising blend of East and West, Venice was neither totally European nor wholly Italian. Byzantine domes, Oriental mosaics and Gothic palaces still evoke this exotic legacy, even if the city enchants us as much for its timelessness and aloofness from modern life.

But contemporary Venice is being bold again, with a sleek bridge over the Grand Canal, a mobile flood barrier nearly completed, designer bed and breakfasts, contemporary wine bars, and a cutting-edge contemporary art museum facing St Mark's. It's a delicate balancing act: visitors also come for the gondolas, the Gothic palaces and the sense of being marooned in a gorgeous Disneyland for grown-ups.

GEOGRAPHY

The sea has always been linked with the city's fortunes and, like the swampy, shallow Venetian lagoon, it is both loved and feared. Situated at the northwestern end of the Adriatic Sea, Venice lies on an archipelago in a crescent-shaped lagoon 50 km (32 miles) in length. Greater Venice stands on 118 flat islets, with its buildings supported by millions of larch poles driven into sediment. Crisscrossing the city is a labyrinth of over 160 canals, spanned by more than 400 bridges. These canals are partly flushed out by the tides that sweep in daily from the Adriatic through three channels that pierce the ring of sand bars (*lidi*) protecting the lagoon. However, given the rising sea levels, Venice has been increasingly swept by sporadic winter floods, hence the demand for a tidal barrier. But environmentalists believe that Venice's problems are a microcosm of those affecting many other cities and that it's not too late to save Venice and the Venetians.

Decorative Venetian mask

NAVIGATING THE CITY

Any visitor to Venice has to confront its unique geography. Exploring the city properly means pounding the canalsides and clambering the many bridges. Travel light and leap on a *vaporetto* (waterbus) when flagging. The ferries ply the Grand Canal, but will also whisk you out to the islands of the Venetian lagoon – from the Lido beaches to the brightly painted houses on Burano, or from Murano's glass showrooms to Torcello's medieval cathedral, set amid remote salt marshes. You can even inspect the controversial mobile flood barrier, which should be fully functioning by 2022. Yet even if the physical threats come from the sea, the social challenges are no less serious. Venice may be mired in its glorious past, with Gothic palaces galore, but it needs to retain its population if it is to stave off its fate as a theme park.

MEET THE VENETIANS

Since the population fell below 60,000, the city has had a rude wake-up call. In its heyday, the city of Venice had 200,000

Gondolier on a break

inhabitants – a figure that fell to 90,000 at the end of the Republic and currently stands at around a mere 54,000. Venice's resident population keeps shrinking, leaving the Venetians an endangered species. Whether craftsmen or boat builders, the locals are struggling to survive in a city dedicated to other people's dreams. Architect Francesco da Mosto worries whether his children will be the last generation to go to school in Venice. Chef Enrica Rocca mocks her neighbourhood as a place in which 'you can buy a mask more easily than milk'.

SUSTAINABLE TOURISM

Tourism has become both the lifeblood and the bane of Venice, with around 22 million tourists a year. This is nothing new: in his 1912 novella *Death in Venice*, Thomas Mann describes the city as 'half fairy tale, half tourist trap'.

A simmering rebellion against exorbitant rents and the creeping colonisation of mask shops and hotels reflects a local backlash against mass tourism. The exponential growth of cruise tourism also threatens to overwhelm the ancient city. There is no magical solution, but pressure groups are calling for more sustainable tourism, backed by investment in culture and crafts. You can now learn to cook with a Venetian countess, or embark on a craft course with Cannaregio artisans.

If you're feeling daring, try kayaking or row standing up, gondolier-style.

Your gift to ordinary Venetians is not simply to daydream your way through the city but to drift a while with them, and to support local culture. Lose yourself in the backwaters and mingle with the Venetians themselves. Whether it's staying in a bed and breakfast or attending a Baroque recital, you are helping Venice survive.

For sustainable shopping, seek out traditional Venetian crafts, from stationery to ceramics, including Murano glass and masks only where the provenance is guaranteed. Chat to master craftsman of paper and bookbinding, Paolo Olbi, and caress the exquisite hand-tooled notebooks that caught Johnny Depp's eye while filming here. Craft shopping is an intimate experience, a secret glimpse of Venetians at their best.

⊙ THE LIONS OF VENICE

Pacific, playful or warlike, lions dominate paintings, sculptures, crests and illuminated manuscripts in Venice; they adorn buildings, bridges, balconies, archways and doorways, with the greatest concentration in the San Marco and Castello districts, closest to the centre of power. Whereas the seated lion represents the majesty of state, the walking lion symbolises Venetian sovereignty over its dominions. The Lion of St Mark bears a traditional greeting of peace and in times of war is depicted with a closed book, as in the arch over the Arsenale gateway. A few lions are shown clutching a drawn sword in one of their paws. The Napoleonic forces were well aware of the symbolism of lions and destroyed many prominent images; as a result, some, such as those on the Gothic gateway to the Palazzo Ducale, are replicas.

A BRIEF HISTORY

It may be hard to believe, but this tiny city was once the centre of the wealthiest, most powerful state in Europe. In its prime, Venice influenced the course of modern history, leaving an incomparable legacy in the shape of the city itself.

EARLY VENETIANS

Although the earliest Venetians were fishermen and boatmen skilled at navigating the shallow lagoon's islands, the first major settlers arrived after the Lombards invaded in AD 568. The invasion led the coastal dwellers to flee to low-lying off-shore islands in the lagoon, such as Torcello and Malamocco, on the string of *lidi*, or barrier beaches, on the Adriatic.

Venetia, or Venezia, was the name of the entire area at the northern end of the Adriatic under the Roman Empire. Venice as we know it developed gradually around a cluster of small islands that remained out of reach of the north Italian Lombard kingdom and were subject only to lose control from the Roman-Byzantine centre at Ravenna, which answered to Constantinople. Around AD 697 the lagoon communities were united under a separate military command, set up at Malamocco, with a *dux* (Latin for leader), or doge, in charge. Though the first doges were probably selected by the lagoon dwellers, they still took orders from the Byzantine emperor.

Patron saint

When St Mark's relics reached Venice c.829, a chapel (the original St Mark's) was built for them next to the Palazzo Ducale. Mark's winged lion emblem was adopted as the symbol of the city.

The Lombards were succeeded on the mainland in 774 by Charlemagne's Frankish army, and in 810 his son Pépin was sent to conquer the communities of the lagoon. Pépin seized the outer island of Malamocco, but the doge and his entourage managed to escape to the safety of the Rivo Alto (High Shore), the future Rialto, where they built a fortress on the site now housing the Palazzo Ducale (Doge's Palace).

St Mark's trademark lion

THE RISE OF THE REPUBLIC

The new city gradually became independent of distant Byzantium, prospering due to tight control of the north Italian river deltas and, later, of the sea itself. Fishing, salt and the lumber and slave trades enriched the city, and rival producers and traders were ruthlessly quashed. From the 9th century, in defiance of the pope and the Byzantine emperor, the Venetians traded with the Islamic world, selling luxuries from Constantinople at a high profit to the rest of Europe. By this time, Venice was no longer a dependency of the Byzantine Empire, and, to underline this, snatched the body of St Mark from Muslim-controlled Alexandria, in Egypt, c.829. Mark replaced the Byzantine saint, Theodore, as the patron of Venice.

Marco Polo leaving Venice

EMPIRE BUILDING

The city's newly founded Arsenale turned out fleets of ever-mightier galleys, enabling Venice to move into the Adriatic, where it warred for decades with its bitter enemy, the Dalmatia. In the year 1000, the Republic scored a significant victory and celebrated it with a 'marriage to the sea' ceremony, which is still re-enacted annually (see page 97). Ships flying St Mark's pennant ranged over the Aegean Sea and the eastern Mediterranean, trading, plundering and bringing back spoils to strengthen the state. Venice soon came to be known as the *Serenissima* (Most Serene Republic), or 'Queen of the Seas'.

From the start of the Crusades in 1095, the Venetians sensed rich pickings. Ideally positioned both politically and geographically between Europe and the East, and with little concern for the spiritual aspect of the campaigns, Venice produced and outfitted ships and equipped knights, often at huge profit.

Crusader armies sacked Constantinople, the greatest repository of the ancient world's treasures, under the 90-year-old Doge Enrico Dandalo in 1204. Among the rich pickings were the four bronze horses that adorn the Basilica di San Marco. By now the Republic was a world power, controlling all the major points along the routes to Egypt and the Crimea.

At the end of the 13th century, the Venetians curbed the power of the doges, evolving into a patrician oligarchy. Eventually, the doges became little more than pampered prisoners in their palace, stripped of every vestige of authority; their primary function was to preside over the Republic's pompous festivities, and after 1310 no major change was made in the constitution until the Republic fell in 1797.

WARS AND INTRIGUE

Venice spent much of the 14th century battling with its rival, Genoa, over the slave and grain trades in the Black Sea. They also fought over the route from the Mediterranean north to Bruges and Antwerp, where spices and other wares could be traded for prized Flemish cloth, English wool and tin. In 1379, during the fourth and final Genoese War, Venice came closer to defeat than at any time in its history: the Genoese fleet, aided by Hungarian and Paduan troops, captured and sank Venetian ships in home waters. When the key port of Chioggia, south of Venice, was taken, the *Serenissima* seemed lost. The Venetians

⌾ MARCO POLO

Venice's most famous citizen opened the eyes of 13th-century Europe to the irresistibly exotic mysteries of Asia. While recent scholarship has thrown some doubt on the authenticity of his story, Marco Polo relates how, for some 20 years, he served the Mongol Emperor Kublai Khan and was the first Westerner permitted to travel about freely in China. When he came back from China, legend has it that nobody recognized him or believed his tales – until he slit the seams of his clothes and precious jewels fell out.

Doge Loredan

retook the port, however, and in 1380 Genoa surrendered, forever finished as a major maritime force.

The 14th century was also a time for domestic difficulties. In 1310 a group of disgruntled aristocrats under Baiamonte Tiepolo tried to seize power and kill the doge, but their revolt was quickly crushed. Worse was to come: between 1347 and 1349 almost half of the city's population of 120,000 was wiped out by the Black Death. A further 20,000 Venetians died in another epidemic in 1382, and over the next three centuries the city was almost never free of plague.

The Republic began to focus attention on its land boundary. As an expanding manufacturing city in the 15th century, it needed food, wood and metal from the nearest possible sources. However, its push along the northern Italian rivers and across the plain of Lombardy soon met with opposition, and the conflicts known as the Lombard Wars began in 1425. The Republic defended its new territory so tenaciously that Milan, Florence and Naples formed an anti-Venice coalition, worried that Venice might take over the entire Italian peninsula.

NEW THREATS IN A GOLDEN AGE

With the dying Byzantine Empire no longer able to buffer Venice against threats from the east, a new rival arose in the shape of the Ottoman Empire. Initially, the young sultan, Mohammed the Conqueror, was not taken seriously, and inadequate forces were sent by the Venetians to protect Constantinople. In 1453 the city fell to the Turks, who played havoc with Venetian trade routes and won a key naval battle at Negroponte in the northern Aegean in 1470. Although Venice was still the leading Mediterranean maritime power, these defeats marked the beginning of a downhill slide.

While its fortunes beyond the lagoon waned, Venetian civilisation reached new heights. No building in the Western world was more sumptuous than the Palazzo Ducale; no church had as many treasures as San Marco. And as artists such as Bellini, Giorgione, Carpaccio, Tintoretto, Veronese and Titian flourished, Andrea Palladio's revolutionary concepts began to shape the future of architecture. Venice was also home to the most complex economy and the richest culture in all of Europe.

Yet the threats to the Republic continued to accumulate. In 1498 Vasco da Gama of Portugal undertook his epic voyage around the Cape of Good Hope to India, opening up new trade routes and putting an end to Venice's spice-trade monopoly. During the same period of prodigious exploration, Christopher Columbus's landfalls on the other side of the Atlantic proved momentous for the Venetian Republic. The axis of power in Europe gradually moved to countries on the Atlantic coast. As trade with the New World mushroomed, the Oriental trade that had long ensured Venetian prosperity fell into decline.

DECLINE AND DECADENCE

After the French invasion of Italy in 1494, Venice sought to further encroach on the latter. However, this international brinkmanship so incensed the rest of Europe that, in 1508, under the auspices of Pope Julius II and the king of Spain, a pan-European organisation, known as the League of Cambrai, was formed

View of the Ducal Palace in Venice by Canaletto

with the aim of destroying the Republic. City after city defected, as the Republic's 20,000-strong mercenary army fell apart. For a while things seemed desperate, but the League itself fell apart through internal struggles, and Venice managed to regain nearly all its territories. However, seven years of war cost the Venetians dearly, putting a stop to their ambitions in Italy. Furthermore, with Charles V's Empire steadily accumulating Italian ground, considerable Venetian diplomacy was needed for the city to preserve its independence.

Around the eastern and southern Mediterranean, the Ottomans surged on, and the Battle of Lepanto, in 1571, finally turned the Turkish tide. The fleet of the Holy League was spearheaded by Venice, but the allies, by now suspicious of Venice, ensured that the city did not profit from this victory; instead of continuing the offensive east, they signed away the Venetian stronghold of Cyprus as part of the peace treaty.

From 1575 to 1577 plague raged again, and the population fell from 150,000 to 100,000. Despite this, and the Republic's diminishing political powers, Venice prospered through the 16th and 17th centuries, aided by the skills and contacts of Jewish refugees from the Italian peninsula and Spain. Music flourished, with Claudio Monteverdi in the 17th century and Antonio Vivaldi in the 18th. Venice's art tradition continued with Tiepolo and Canaletto, and the playwright Carlo Goldoni's new adaptations of *commedia dell'arte* broke exciting ground. If the city was a fading world power, it fast warmed to its new role as the playground of Europe, staging extravagant carnival balls and becoming notorious for gambling.

THE END OF THE REPUBLIC

By the end of the 18th century the Venetians knew that Napoleon was on the warpath but were simply too weak to stop him. He entered the city, demanding that the government turn its power over to a democratic council under French military protection. In 1797 the last doge, Ludovico Manin, abdicated, the Great Council voted to dissolve itself, and the *Serenissima* was no more. Napoleon's troops looted and destroyed the Arsenale, but they stayed in Venice for only five months, until their emperor was forced to relinquish it to Austrian control. However, in 1805, Napoleon returned, having defeated the Austrians at Austerlitz, and he made the city part of his short-lived Kingdom of Italy.

After Waterloo, the Austrians again occupied Venice, and stayed for more than 50 years, until 1866. Although the Austrians were despised by the Venetians, they did restore to the city most of the artistic booty taken by Napoleon. In 1846 they linked Venice to the mainland for the first time, erecting an unsightly railway bridge. In 1848, the Venetians rose up under revolutionary leader Daniele Manin and ousted the

Casa or palazzo?

Until the late 17th century the Palazzo Ducale was the only building in Venice that was allowed to be called a *palazzo*. Other splendid mansions were called simply Casa (house), shortened to Ca'. Many families did not bother to rename their houses *palazzi* once it was permitted, hence Ca' d'Oro, Ca' da Mosto and so on.

Austrian garrison; however, their provisional republic fell the following year. In 1866, after Austria's defeat by Prussia, the Venetians voted overwhelmingly to join the new Kingdom of Italy.

THE CITY TODAY

Venice remained largely unscathed by two world wars; more damaging was the pollution caused by an industrial port and oil refinery built at Porto Marghera in the 1920s. Equally serious was the severe flooding in November 1966, which led to the setting up of local and international organisations to restore Venetian artworks and palaces and to protect the city.

MOSE, a controversial mobile flood barrier that is expected to be completed by 2022, will eventually regulate water at the three entrance points to the lagoon, to prevent the sporadic flooding of the city. Until then, winter floods see citizens and visitors resort to boots and duckboards. The Venice in Peril Fund (www.veniceinperil.org) supports the mobile barrier project, whilst admitting that it doesn't address the chronic issue of rising water levels and the degradation of the lagoon.

High water *(aqua alta)* is a seasonal phenomenon, when a combination of high tides and a strong Sirocco wind lead to an inrush of water into the Venetian Lagoon, and flooding in the city centre. High water happens in autumn and winter when air pressure is particularly low or when the Sirocco wind is blowing. Given that virtually all of Venice lies about 100cm (3ft) above sea level, it takes an exceptional tide of over 140cm (4.5ft) to affect large parts of the city.

There are claims that by 2100 Venice could be the most famous fatality of climate change. Others, like writer Jonathan Keates, see chinks of hope: "Venice's very existence derives from a simple human yearning to make things happen against the odds."

HISTORICAL LANDMARKS

6th century AD Refugees fleeing barbarians settle in the lagoon.

696 Election of Paoluccio Anafesto as the first doge.

829 The body of St Mark, stolen from Alexandria, is smuggled to Venice.

991–1008 Doge Pietro Orseolo II reigns. Commercial advantages are gained from Byzantium, and a sea battle is won against Dalmatia.

1104 The Arsenale is founded.

1202–4 Venice diverts the Fourth Crusade and sacks Constantinople.

1347–9 Nearly half the city's population wiped out by the Black Death.

1405 Venice takes Verona from Milan.

1423 Election of Doge Francesco Foscari begins Venetian expansion to Bergamo and Brescia and on to parts of Cremona.

1453 The Turks take Constantinople, heralding the expansion of the Ottoman Empire in Europe.

1571 Resounding victory against the Turks at Lepanto.

1797 Napoleonic troops enter Venice, and the Republic comes to an end.

1815 The Treaty of Vienna places the Veneto under Austrian control.

1848 Under Daniele Manin, Venice rebels against Austria.

1866 Venice becomes part of unified Italy.

1914–18 World War I. More than 600 bombs are dropped on Venice.

1966 Disastrous flooding leads to the launch of an international appeal.

1979 The Venice Carnival is revived and goes from strength to strength.

1996 Most severe floods for 30 years; fire at La Fenice opera house.

2008 The Calatrava Bridge is erected over the Grand Canal.

2009 The Punta della Dogana Contemporary Art Centre opens.

2013 The population of Venice falls to under 60,000.

2014 Venice's mayor Giorgio Orsoni and 35 others are put under arrest or investigation for allegedly siphoning off millions of euros from the MOSE flood barrier project.

2018 Serious floods occur with *acqua alta* (high water) of 156cm (5.1ft).

2019 After a huge cruise ship crashes into a wharf and a tourist boat injures five people, residents demand a ban on these ships in Venice's lagoon.

2022 MOSE, the system of 78 mobile dams, is due to be fully operational.

Gondola on a canal

WHERE TO GO

More like a stage set than a city, Venice has captivated visitors for centuries. *La Serenissima* dazzles and mesmerises, but also bewilders. Its singularity disorients the unprepared, but its uniqueness makes it a wonder of the world. Piazza San Marco is like a magnet, no matter your intention, you are inexorably drawn back, directed by the authoritative yellow *'per San Marco'* signs that mark the main thoroughfares. It is no hardship to return. The beautifully proportioned square that Napoleon termed 'the finest drawing room in Europe' is home to the great Basilica, the Doge's Palace and gracious cafés.

Venice is traditionally divided into six *sestieri* (districts). The obvious place to start is San Marco, with its famous church and piazza. To the east is Castello, home to several major churches and the Arsenale. South and west of San Marco, on the other side of the Grand Canal, is Dorsoduro with its art galleries, while inside the northern bend of the Grand Canal are San Polo and Santa Croce districts, centred on the Rialto. Finally, further north, with the train station and former Jewish Ghetto, is Cannaregio.

Stand on a little humpbacked bridge, far from the Grand Canal, and all you'll hear is the water lapping against the mossy walls, or the swish of a gondola that appears out of nowhere. Despite its watery character, most of the city is best explored on foot, with the occasional boat trip adding a new perspective or whisking you to the far corners of the lagoon.

SAN MARCO

The magnet is always San Marco, home to several of the city's main landmarks. But do dip in and out of the square, as Venetians do, before exploring the rest of Venice. Despite its allure, this ceremonial district has little in common with the intimacy of other less well-known districts, let alone with the lagoon islands.

PIAZZA SAN MARCO

The main square in Venice, **Piazza San Marco** ❶, is a pulsating spot. The square was originally home to a monastic garden with a canal running through it, but since its transformation in the 12th and 13th centuries it has been the religious and political centre of the city. The Piazza has always pulled in the crowds – at the peak of the Republic's powers, some of the world's most spectacular processions, such as the one depicted in Gentile Bellini's celebrated painting at the Accademia (see page 53), were staged here. Victorious commanders returning home from the Genoese or Turkish wars were fêted in front of the Basilica with grand parades, while vendors on the square sold sweets and snacks, much as they do today. And under the arcades, Venetians and tourists have promenaded and been enchanted by elegant shops for centuries.

Yet despite all its pomp and circumstance and hustle and bustle, the Piazza remains a very civilised place. Dubbed by Napoleon the 'finest drawing room in Europe', it is elegantly proportioned, with colonnades on three sides, and fringed with exquisite monuments (most dating from the 16th and 17th centuries). Interestingly, the 'square' is actually a trapezoid, with uneven pavements sloping

When to visit

Visit Venice in May or October if you can – the crowds at Easter and from June to September can be frustrating. Christmas in Venice has also become fashionable; though the city can be dank and cold in winter, it takes on a rather mystical beauty at this time.

Basilica di San Marco

slightly downwards towards the Basilica. Its trachyte (volcanic rock) paving strips are more than 250 years old and lie over five or six earlier layers of tiles from the mid-13th century.

BASILICA DI SAN MARCO

Blending Eastern and Western elements, the **Basilica di San Marco** ❷ (St Mark's Basilica; www.basilicasanmarco.it; Mon–Sat 9.30am–5pm, Sun and hols 2–4.30pm, mid-Apr–late Oct Sun and hols until 5pm; leave bags in the Ateneo San Basso, Calle San Basso 315/A; free) is an exquisite, sumptuous shrine, encapsulating the old Republic's vision of itself as the successor to Constantinople. Despite the sloping irregular floors, an eclectic mix of styles both inside and out, the five low domes of totally unequal proportions and some 500 non-matching columns, San Marco still manages to convey a sense of grandeur as well as a jewel-like delicacy.

Jump the queue

To avoid the long queues
for the Basilica di San
Marco reserve in advance
at www.venetoinside.com.
Take your reservation to
the special entrance for
those with bookings.

The church was originally built in AD 830 as a chapel for the doges and as a resting place for the remains of St Mark, which had just been stolen from Alexandria by two Venetian adventurers (see page 15). According to legend, they hid the body in a consignment of salted pork; Muslim customs officials, forbidden by their religion from eating or coming in contact with pork, did not do a thorough search and let the relics slip through their fingers. Not only were the body and many of the adornments in the Basilica stolen from the East but most of the church's columns were also brought back as booty from forays into the Levant. The Basilica became the Republic's shrine as well as the coronation place of its doges. However, the original, largely wooden church burned down in 976, and the Basilica we see today was constructed between 1063 and 1094; its exterior was then lavishly decorated with marble and ornamentation over the next three centuries.

The narthex

The small porch at the entrance to the cathedral (the narthex) gives visitors their first sight of the fabulous **mosaics** that are a predominant feature of the church's interior. Described by the poet W.B. Yeats as 'God's holy fire', they are said to cover a total area of around 0.5 hectares (1 acre). The narthex mosaics date from the 13th century and are among the most spectacular in the whole Basilica; they depict such Old Testament events as the Creation and the story of Noah's ark. The mosaics are at their best from 11.30am–12.45pm daily when the cathedral is illuminated.

Museo Marciano

The staircase immediately to the right of the main entrance leads to a small museum, the **Museo Marciano** (daily late Oct–mid-Apr 9.45am–4.45pm, mid-Apr–late Oct 9.35am–5pm), housing some of the San Marco's finest treasures. The star attraction is the world's only surviving ancient *quadriga* (four horses abreast), known as the **Cavalli di San Marco** (The Horses of St Mark) and cast around AD 200, either in Rome or Greece. At one time, the horses were believed to have crowned Trajan's Arch in Rome, but they were later moved to the imperial hippodrome in Constantinople, where Doge Dandolo claimed them as spoils of war in 1204, bringing them back to Venice. After guarding the shipyard of the Venetian Arsenale for a while, the *quadriga* was moved to the front of the cathedral, becoming almost as symbolic of the city as St Mark's trademark lion.

In 1378 the rival republic of Genoa boasted that it would 'bridle those unbridled horses', but it never succeeded. Napoleon managed to corral them, however, taking them to Paris to stand on the Place du Carrousel adjacent to the Louvre for 13 years. When Venice fell under Austrian rule, the Austrians restored the horses to San Marco, where they remained until World War I, when the

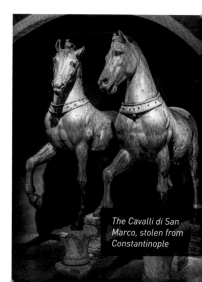

The Cavalli di San Marco, stolen from Constantinople

Italian government moved them to Rome. During World War II they were moved again, this time into the nearby countryside. After the war, they were returned to the Basilica, although the ones on display at the front of the cathedral are only replicas – the original *quadriga* was moved inside to protect it against corrosion from air pollution. The Venetians have vowed that the horses will never be allowed to leave their city again.

The galleries in which the museums are situated provide good views of the interior; while outside on the Loggia dei Cavalli you can look down on Piazza San Marco and the adjacent piazzetta.

The Treasury and High Altar

Located just off the baptistery on the Basilica's right-hand side is the **Tesoro** (Treasury; late Oct–mid-Apr Mon–Sat 9.45am–4.45pm, Sun and hols 2–4.30pm, mid-Apr–late Oct Mon–Sat 9.35am–5pm, Sun and hols 2–5pm), where you can see further riches looted from Constantinople at the time of the Fourth Crusade (1204). Close by is the **Altare Maggiore** (High Altar), which bears a *ciborium* (canopy) mounted on four alabaster columns dating from the 7th or 8th century; sculpted scenes from the lives of Christ and the Virgin Mary adorn the altar. In the illuminated grating is a sarcophagus containing the relics of St Mark.

Dress code

Visitors in short skirts or shorts will not be allowed entry to Venice's churches, especially the Basilica di San Marco. Shoulders and backs must also be covered.

The Pala d'Oro

Behind the altar is one of Christendom's greatest treasures, the **Pala d'Oro** (same as the treasury), a gold, bejewelled altar screen featuring dozens of scenes from the Bible. Originally crafted in the 12th century, the screen was embellished and enlarged on the doges' orders until it reached its present stage in the mid-14th century. Its exquisitely wrought golden frame holds the Venetian equivalent of the Crown Jewels: 1,300 pearls, 400 garnets, 300 sapphires, 300 emeralds, 90 amethysts, 75 balas rubies, 15 rubies, four topazes and two cameos.

The only drawback to the fabulous splendour of the Pala d'Oro is that it attracts hordes of sightseers. The best way to try and beat the crowds is to visit either early in the morning, before day-trippers and tour groups have arrived, or late in the afternoon, after they have left.

CAMPANILE DI SAN MARCO

For breathtaking views of Piazza San Marco and the city, ascend the **Campanile di San Marco** (St Mark's Bell Tower; www.basili casanmarco.it; daily 1–15 Apr 9am–5.30pm, mid-Apr–Sept

The Campanile

8.30am–9pm, Oct 9.30am–6pm, Nov–Mar 9.30am–4.45pm), at 100m (335ft) Venice's tallest building, which over the years has served as a lighthouse, gun turret and belfry. Within less than a minute a lift takes you to the top, where the exotic domes of the Basilica, the splendid wedge-shaped tip of the Dorsoduro (marking the start of the Grand Canal), the island church of San Giorgio Maggiore and the terracotta-coloured tiles of the ancient city roofscape are spread beneath your feet. The scene looks much the same now as it did over 200 years ago when the German writer J.W. von Goethe came here for his first view of the sea. It may well even look the same as four centuries ago when, according to local lore, Galileo brought the doge up here to show off his new telescope. Intriguingly, not a single canal can be seen from the Campanile.

However, this most potent symbol of the city is not the original tower, which collapsed into the Piazza on 14 July 1902. Fortunately, the old building creaked and groaned so much in advance that everyone knew what was coming – numerous bell towers in Venice have fallen down over the centuries, so the locals were used to it and knew to keep their distance; the eventual collapse caused no injury. Contrary to the 'evidence' supplied on cleverly faked postcards on sale throughout the city, the moment was not caught on film.

The city council quickly decided to rebuild the bell tower 'as it was, where it was', and precisely 1,000 years after the erection of the original Campanile, on 25 April 1912 a new, lighter version was inaugurated. However, like many Venetian bell towers, this one is already starting to lean.

PIAZZETTA DEI LEONCINI

The small square situated to the left as you face the Basilica is known as the **Piazzetta dei Leoncini**, after the two marble lions that have been here since 1722. On the side of the Basilica facing the Piazzetta is the tomb of Daniele Manin, the leader of Venice's revolt against Austria and the subsequent, short-lived Venetian Republic of 1848–9. A descendent of a family from the Venetian Ghetto, the heroic Manin was reinterred in this site of unequalled honour after the end of the Austrian Occupation in 1866, along with his wife and children – none of the doges were granted such a splendid resting place.

TORRE DELL'OROLOGIO

The Campanile is not the Piazza's only notable bell tower – the graceful **Torre dell'Orologio** (Clock Tower; tel: 848082000; www.visitmuve.it; tours by appointment only, in English Mon–Wed at 11am and noon, Thu–Sun at 2pm and 3pm), features a splendid **zodiacal clock** that shows the time in both Arabic and Roman numerals and has been ticking for over 500 years. On Epiphany in January and through Ascension week in May three bright-eyed Magi and a trumpeting angel swing out from the face of the clock tower on the stroke of every hour and, stiffly bowing, ceremoniously rotate around a gilded Madonna.

At the top of the tower, two scantily clad North African bronze figures use hammers to strike a bell. According to Venetian legend, stroking the figures' exposed nether regions

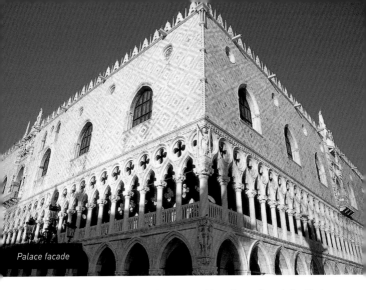
Palace facade

confers sexual potency for a year. Venetians also claim that a workman was knocked off the top of the tower in the 19th century by one of the hammers – perhaps a kind of revenge for the impertinence that the statues have to endure.

PROCURATIE VECCHIE AND NUOVE

Adjacent to the Torre dell'Orologio is the colonnaded **Procuratie Vecchie**, built in the 16th century as a home for the Procurators of San Marco (state officers charged with the administration of the *sestieri*, or Venetian districts). Below it is one of Venice's two most famous cafés, the Caffè Quadri (www.alajmo.it), favoured haunt of the Austrians during their occupation of the city in the 19th century.

The church of San Geminiano once stood at the far end of the Piazza opposite the Basilica, but in 1807 Napoleon ordered it to be demolished in order to make way for a wing joining the two sides of the square. On the facade of this wing, known as the **Ala Napoleonica** (Napoleon's Wing), there are several statues of Roman emperors and a central niche originally intended for a statue of Napoleon himself but pointedly left empty.

Opposite the Procuratie Vecchie is the **Procuratie Nuove**, built between 1582 and 1640 as a new home for the Procurators, and later occupied by Napoleon as a royal palace. The Museo Correr (see page 40) now occupies most of the upper floors of this building and the adjacent Ala Napoleonica. Below the Procuratie Nuove, on the side of the square facing Caffè Quadri, is the Piazza's other famous café, Florian (www.caffeflorian. com). Founded in 1720, but with a mid-19th-century interior, it may be the oldest continuously operating café in the world.

PALAZZO DUCALE

For nine centuries the magnificent **Palazzo Ducale ❸** (Doge's Palace; www.visitmuve.it; daily Apr–Oct Sun–Thu 8.30am–9pm, Fri–Sat until 11pm, Nov–Mar 8.30am–7pm, last entrance half an hour before closing time) was the seat of the Republic, serving as a council chamber, law court and prison, as well as the residence of most of Venice's doges. The Palazzo was first built in fortress-like Byzantine style in the 9th century and partially replaced 500 years later by a Gothic structure. The architects of this massive structure, with peach-and-white patterning in its brick facade, achieved an incredible delicacy by balancing the bulk of the building above two floors of Gothic arcades. The ravages inflicted by three devastating fires have necessitated some extensive reconstruction work over the centuries.

The palace's 15th-century ceremonial entrance, the **Porta della Carta** (Paper Gate), is a masterpiece of late Gothic stonework. Its name may derive from the fact that the doge's decrees were affixed here, or from the professional scribes who set up nearby. On the left, note the four curious dark brown figures of the Tetrarchs (also known as the 'Four Moors'), variously said to represent the Roman emperor Diocletian and associates, or four Saracen robbers who tried to loot the Basilica's *Treasury* through the wall behind them.

Visits start at the Porta del Frumento on the lagoon side of the palace. The **Museo dell' Opera** by the entrance houses some of the original carved capitals from the palazzo's loggias. Inside the courtyard is the impressive ceremonial stairway, the **Scala dei Giganti**, named after Sansovino's colossal statues of Neptune and Mars (symbolising, respectively, Venetian sea and land powers). Visitors use the only slightly less grandiose **Scala d'Oro** (Golden Staircase), which was built during the 16th century to designs by Jacopo Sansovino.

The interior

The main tour of the palace begins in the state rooms, in which the business of the Republic was once conducted. This part of the complex is home to some of the finest paintings in the ducal collection. On the walls in front of and behind you as you enter the **Anticollegio** are four allegories by Tintoretto, combining images of pagan gods and the four seasons to suggest that Venice is favoured at all times. Jacob Bassano's *Jacob Returning to Canaan* is on the wall opposite the windows, on your right. To the left of it is Veronese's masterpiece, *The Rape of Europa*.

Proceed on to the **Sala del Collegio**, where the doges received ambassadors. Next is the **Sala del Senato** where the Venetian ruling council (made up of the doge, his advisors, members of the judiciary and senators) formulated policy.

The next room is the **Sala del Consiglio dei Dieci**, the meeting room of the Council of Ten. The Ten (who actually numbered up to 17) were a high-ranking group that met on matters of state security and acquired a reputation similar to that of the secret police. A letter box in the form of a lion's mouth, for the use of citizens who wished to inform the Ten of anything untoward, can be seen in the next room.

On the public route, the palace's somewhat menacing aura is confirmed by a splendid private armoury, in which some extremely gruesome weapons are displayed.

The route then leads down to the first-floor state rooms. The most resplendent of all, is the **Sala del Maggior Consiglio** (Great Council Chamber), a vast hall where Venetian citizens assembled to elect doges and debate state policies in the early days of the Republic. Later, only the nobles convened here. The hall was built to hold an assembly of up to 1,700, but by the mid-16th century this figure had increased to around 2,500. Covering the whole of one end wall is Tintoretto's *Paradiso*, based on Dante's masterpiece, and undertaken by the artist (with the assistance of his son) while he was in his seventies. At 7m by 22m (23ft by

The Bridge of Sighs

72ft), it is the largest old master oil painting in the world, containing some 350 human figures. Adorning the ceiling is Veronese's *Apotheosis of Venice*, which captures the ideal civic conception of Venice as serene, prosperous, elegant and self-assured. Portraits of 76 doges (several of which are little more than artistic guesswork) line the cornice beneath the ceiling. Conspicuously absent is the 14th-century doge, Marin Falier – a black veil marks his intended place of honour, and a notice tells us that he was beheaded for treason in 1355.

From here the tour takes you to the criminal courts and the Prigioni Nuove (New Prisons), which are reached by the legendary **Bridge of Sighs** (Ponte dei Sospiri). Teasingly, it was once dubbed 'bridge of signs' as it was shrouded in billboards for so long. Now restored, the baroque stone bridge, built in 1614, was given its more evocative name by Lord Byron who wrote: 'I stood in Venice on the Bridge of Sighs, a palace and a prison on each hand'. The idea that condemned prisoners sighed at their last glance of Venice when crossing the bridge derives more from romantic fiction than hard fact, as it was petty criminals who would have made the journey at that time. The bridge has two parallel passageways, each leading to different court and interrogation rooms, with small, dark cells on the other side, which are relatively civilised by medieval standards.

PIAZZETTA SAN MARCO

If Piazza San Marco is the drawing room of Venice, the smaller **Piazzetta San Marco** is its vestibule. The two soaring granite columns dominating the piazzetta were stolen from the East and hoisted upright here in 1172. They haven't moved since, although a third column apparently fell into the sea.

On top of one of the columns is Venice's original patron saint, St Theodore; on the other stands what must be the strangest looking of the city's many stone lions – not really a lion at all but a *chimera*, a mythical hybrid beast (you can see it most clearly from the balcony of the Palazzo Ducale). Even though its exact origin is unknown, it is thought to be of Eastern provenance and may be up to 2,200 years old.

Nowadays the area bustles with tourists, but between the 15th and mid-18th centuries it was a place of execution. One of the more creative punishments involved torturing the prisoner, burning them on a raft, dragging them through the streets and finally putting them to death between the columns.

⊙ SECRET TOURS OF THE PALACE

The Itinerari Segreti is a fascinating guided tour (minimum two people; in English daily at 9.55am, 10.45am and 11.35am), which gives access to secret parts of the Doge's Palace that are normally off limits to visitors. The tour takes around 1 hour 15 minutes and includes the torture chamber and the cell from which Casanova, one of Venice's most notorious citizens, escaped in 1775. The tour ticket also gives access to the rest of the palace. Advance bookings can be made until two days before the visit (tel: 041-427 30892; www.visitmuve.it) or, if still available, on the day by asking at the information desk.

Gran Caffè Chioggia on Piazzetta San Marco

MUSEO CORRER AND MUSEO ARCHEOLOGICO

There are two museums on Piazza San Marco, both of which are usually not too crowded. The **Museo Correr** ❹ (www.visit muve.it; daily Apr–Oct 10am–7pm, Nov–Mar 10.30am–5pm) occupies some 70 rooms of the Ala Napoleonica and Procuratie Nuove. It is home to the city museum and contains artefacts from virtually every aspect of Venice's history. It houses a fine collection of 14th- to 16th-century Venetian paintings, including a room of works by Jacopo Bellini and his sons, Giovanni and Gentile. Vittorie Carpaccio's *Two Venetian Noblewomen*, traditionally and erroneously known as *The Courtesans*, is also displayed here. Other highlights include sculpture by Canova, wonderful old globes and incredible stilt-like platform shoes worn by 15th-century Venetian courtesans.

The **Museo Archeologico** (Archaeological Museum; http:// polomusealeveneto.beniculturali.it; daily Apr–Oct 10am–7pm,

Nov–Mar 10am–5pm), is accessed through Museo Correr. It occupies part of the lavish 16th-century building opposite the Palazzo Ducale on Piazzetta San Marco. The core collection here consists of Greek and Roman sculpture bequeathed by Cardinal Grimani in 1523, a gift that influenced generations of Venetian artists who came to study here. Among the Roman busts, medals, coins, cameos and portraits are Greek originals and Roman copies, including a 5th-century Hellenistic *Persephone*.

BIBLIOTECA MARCIANA

In the other part of the building opposite the Palazzo Ducale, and likewise accessed through Museo Correr, is the **Biblioteca Nazionale Marciana** (National Library of St Mark; daily Apr–Oct 10am–7pm, Nov–Mar 10am–5pm; free guided tours in Italian only by appointment, second Sun of the month at 2.30pm; book at www.venezia-arte.com), also known as the Libreria Sansoviniana after its architect Jacopo Sansovino. Palladio described it as 'the richest building since antiquity'. The magnificent main hall of the original library is decorated with paintings by Veronese, Tintoretto and other leading artists of the time.

Just a few yards behind the library are the **Giardinetti Reali** (Royal Gardens). The best tourist information office (see page 125) is in the neighbouring Venice Pavilion, with another at the southwest exit of Piazza San Marco.

Museum pass

Keen sightseers can cut costs by purchasing a San Marco Square Museum Ticket at www.visitmuve.it, tel: 848082000. This covers the Doge's Palace, Museo Correr, Museo Archeologico and Biblioteca Marciana.

ALSO IN SAN MARCO

If you have more time to explore San Marco *sestiere,* there is an intriguing tower, an opera house and a Gothic church within a few minutes' walk of Piazza San Marco.

Hidden in a maze of alleys between Calle Vida and Calle Contarini, close to Campo Manin, is **Palazzo Contarini del Bovolo** (www.gioiellinascostidivenezia.it; daily 10am–6pm), a late-Gothic palace renowned for its romantic arcaded staircase, the **Scala del Bovolo** ❺. *Bovolo* means 'snail-shell' in Venetian dialect and fittingly describes this graceful spiral staircase, which is linked to loggias of brick and smooth white stone.

La Fenice (visite@festfenice.com; www.teatrolafenice.it; open for 45-minute tours from 9.30am–6pm), the city's main opera house, is located on Campo San Fantin, west of Piazza San Marco. One of the world's loveliest opera auditoria, it was almost completely destroyed by fire in 1838, but rose again 'like a phoenix' *(fenice)*, rebuilt almost exactly. After fire struck again in 1996, the theatre has once again been restored to its former glory and the latest fire precautions installed.

The Gothic **Santo Stefano** church (www.chorusvenezia.org; Mon–Sat 10.30am–4.30pm), located on Campo Santo Stefano, west of the opera house, is a large, airy

Gondolas moored along the quay

structure decorated with rich ornamentation and works by Tintoretto.

CASTELLO

The eastern region of Venice, Castello is the largest of the city's *sestieri*. The name derives from a former 8th century castle built on the island of San Pietro in the east. Castello is home to the Arsenale, where the great Venetian galleys were built, the fine Gothic church

The perfectly proportioned Scala del Bovolo

of Santi Giovanni e Paolo and the Scuola di San Giorgio degli Schiavoni with its exquisite frieze of paintings by Carpaccio.

ALONG THE WATERFRONT

There are few more stately waterfronts in the world than that of Venice's splendid *riva* (quay), which curves gently away from San Marco towards the *sestiere* of Castello. The first section, the **Riva degli Schiavoni** (Quay of the Slavs), begins in front of the Palazzo Ducale. The bustling quay takes its name from the Dalmatian merchants who used to tie up their boats here – vessels laden with wares from the East. This is still a cosmopolitan spot, though less exotic than in its heyday. Boats still moor here, too: *vaporetti* (waterbuses or ferries) at the busy landing stage of San Zaccaria and fleets of gondolas waiting to tempt tourists.

After the Palazzo Ducale, the next sight you'll see (with your back to the waterfront) is the Bridge of Sighs. A little further on

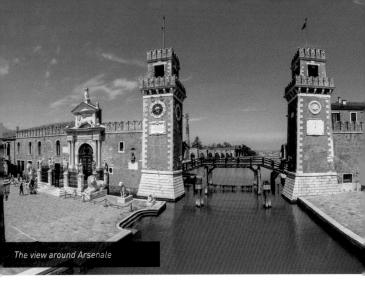
The view around Arsenale

is the red **Palazzo Dandolo**, now the legendary **Hotel Danieli** (www.marriott.com), with a lavish neo-Gothic lobby. When Proust stayed here, he declared, 'When I went to Venice I found that my dream had become – incredibly but quite simply – my address'. The Danieli was also the scene of an unhappy love affair between the writers George Sand and Alfred de Musset in 1883.

A little further on, after the colonnaded Ponte del Vin, the second turning to the left leads away from the waterfront to a quiet *campo* overlooked by the splendid 16th-century church of **San Zaccaria** ❻ (Mon–Sat 10am–noon, 4–6pm, Sun only pm). Supposedly the last resting place of Zaccharias (the father of John the Baptist), whose body lies in the right aisle, this Gothic-Renaissance masterpiece features Giovanni Bellini's celebrated *Madonna and Child*. The side chapels have splendid glowing altarpieces, and the eerie, permanently flooded

8th-century crypt, where several early doges rest in watery graves, is one of the most atmospheric spots in the city.

Back on the waterfront, continue eastwards for the church of **La Pietà** (www.pietavenezia.org; Tue–Sun 10am–6pm), a handsome building with a fine ceiling painting by Giambattista Tiepolo. It is known as 'Vivaldi's church', after Antonio Vivaldi who was concertmaster here from 1705 to 1740.

Carry on past the statue of King Vittorio Emanuele II and you'll notice the crowds starting to thin out. By the time you reach the Arsenale *vaporetto* stop, just a short distance from the Palazzo Ducale, the crowds will probably have dispersed completely, even in high season.

THE ARSENALE

For 700 years, before Napoleon's invasion in the late 18th century, the Republic's galleys and galleons were built at the **Arsenale** ❼ (part of the Arsenal open Mon–Fri 10am–5pm; guided tours June–Nov Mon 10am, by appointment only; tel: 041-521 8828), once the greatest shipyard in the world. Dante visited it, and used the images of its workers toiling amid cauldrons of boiling pitch as the inspiration for his *Inferno*. *Arsenale*, originally from the Arabic for 'house of industry', is one of those Venetian coinages that have passed into universal usage. The yard also originated the concept of the assembly line. Output was prodigious.

One of the yard's proudest achievements came in 1574, while Henri III of France was visiting Venice. In the time it took for the French king to get through his state banquet at the Palazzo Ducale, the workers at the Arsenale had constructed a fully equipped galley from scratch, ready for the king's inspection.

Today, there's little to remind visitors of those heady days. Napoleon destroyed the Arsenale in 1797, and although it was rebuilt by the Austrians, operations here ceased in 1917. The shipyard is now mainly used by the navy, and as the nerve centre for the building of MOSE, the new mobile barrier. Some sections serve as art exhibition spaces during La Biennale (see box) and as venues for concerts. At the entrance visitors can only admire the impressive 15th-century gateway, guarded by a motley collection of white stone lions, all stolen from ancient Greek sites. The two on the river side are believed to date back to the 6th century BC.

MUSEO STORICO NAVALE

The nearest you will get to the spirit of the age is in the **Museo Storico Navale** (Naval History Museum; www.marina.difesa. it; daily Apr–Oct 10am–6pm, Nov–Mar until 5pm). For many visitors the star attraction is the model of the last *Bucintoro*, the gilded barge that was used by the doge on state occasions, although entire sections of other state barges and warships are also on show. If open, don't miss the atmospheric

⊙ LA BIENNALE

Established in 1895, Venice's Biennale (www.labiennale.org) is one of the oldest, most important contemporary art jamborees in the world. Nowadays it takes place in odd numbered years, (the architectural Biennale is held on even years) between June and November. It is held in several main locations – in the Arsenale, where the restored Corderie (rope factory) is the main venue, and in the Giardini Pubblici, where there are around 40 pavilions. Each pavilion is sponsored by a different country, offering a chance for avant-garde art, often with wry political comment. Elsewhere, on the Zattere waterfront behind La Salute, the former salt warehouses have become another showcase for contemporary art.

annexe housed in the old **naval sheds** close to the Arsenale entrance, on the right-hand side of the river, where a range of ships is on display.

Whether heading for the Biennale exhibition or just wandering, it's worth coming this far simply for the splendid views back towards the Palazzo Ducale. Sightseeing as such is subservient to waterfront charm in the untouristy neighbourhood of Eastern Castello.

Lion guarding the Arsenale

SCUOLA DI SAN GIORGIO DEGLI SCHIAVONI

Returning to La Pietà, take the alley beside the church, turn right at Salizzada dei Greci and left after the canal for the **Scuola di San Giorgio degli Schiavoni** (Mon 1.30–5.30pm, Tue–Sat 9.30am–5.30pm, Sun until 1.30pm). The five Venetian *scuole* were craft guilds of laymen under the banner of a particular saint, and this one was founded in 1451 as the guildhall of the city's Dalmatian merchants. In the early 16th century these Slavs *(Schiavoni)*, prospering from trade with the East, commissioned Vittorio Carpaccio to decorate their hall. His nine pictures, completed between 1502 and 1508, decorate the lower floor and depict the lives of the three Dalmatian patron saints: Jerome, Tryphone and George. Note Carpaccio's gory *St George and the Dragon*.

SANTA MARIA FORMOSA

Return to Salizzada dei Greci and follow the flow west across the Rio dei Greci for the Fondamenta dell'Osmarin. A right turn at Calle Rota will take you up to the lively **Campo Santa Maria Formosa** and the 15th-century church of the same name (www.chorusvenezia.org; Mon–Sat 10.30am–4.30pm), which is noted for its altarpiece by Palma il Vecchio.

SANTI GIOVANNI E PAOLO (SAN ZANIPOLO)

Commonly known as **San Zanipolo** ❽ (names are often slurred together in the Venetian dialect), this church (www.basilica santigiovannipaolo.it; Mon–Sat 9am–6pm, Sun noon–6pm) is one of the largest in Venice after San Marco, disputing second place with its great Gothic sister, the Frari (see page 65). The church is located on Campo Santi Giovanni e Paolo, north of Campo Santa Maria Formosa, reached via the café-lined Calle Lunga Santa Maria Formosa. The huge brick church was completed in 1430 for the Dominican Order and is known nowadays as Venice's Pantheon, as such a large number of doges (25 in all) and dignitaries of the Republic lie within. Like the Frari, the church is cavernous, with graphic sculptures adorning its tombs. The church's treasures include an early polyptych by Giovanni Bellini in the right-hand nave.

San Zanipolo shares the *campo* with the late 15th-century **Scuola Grande di San Marco** (now the civic hospital; www.scuolagrandesanmarco.it; Tue–Sat and 1st Sun of the month 9.30am–5.30pm) and a magnificent 15th-century equestrian **statue of Bartolomeo Colleoni** by Andrea Verrochio and Alessandro Leopardi. The subject is the mercenary military leader who worked in the service of Venice for many years and left a large legacy to the city on condition that his statue would be raised 'on the Square of San Marco'. The leaders of the

Stalls in Campo Santa Maria Formosa

Republic, who had never erected statues to any of their leaders or permitted cults of personality, wanted the legacy but could not conceive of erecting a statue to a mercenary soldier in Piazza San Marco. As a compromise, Colleoni's statue was placed in the square of the Scuola Grande di San Marco – the rather tenuous San Marco association presumably saved the municipal conscience.

SANTA MARIA DEI MIRACOLI

West of Santi Giovanni e Paolo, hidden amid a warren of canals and houses, lies the beautifully restored church of **Santa Maria dei Miracoli** (www.chorusvenezia.org; Mon–Sat 10.30am–4.30pm) a popular choice for Venetian weddings. Built from 1481 to 1489 by the Lombardo family of inventive stonemasons who also created the trompe-l'œil facade of the Scuola Grande di San Marco, the church has exquisite marble veneers on its inner and outer walls and an arched ceiling decorated with 50 portraits of prophets and saints.

DORSODURO

Dorsoduro encompasses the section of Venice that lies just across the Grand Canal from San Marco. As a name, 'Dorsoduro' is familiar to few first-time visitors, yet most will fall for this picturesque *sestiere*. It is home to Venice's finest art gallery, the Accademia and to the iconic Santa Maria della Salute basilica.

Chic Dorsoduro is the artiest *sestiere*, with beguiling walks along the Zattere quayside, and bohemian backwaters with a gondola boatyard and earthy Giudecca counterpointed by the grandstanding art and architecture of La Salute, the Accademia and the Guggenheim collection.

Santa Maria dei Miracoli

THE ACCADEMIA

The **Gallerie dell'Accademia** ❾ (Mon 8.15am–2pm, Tue–Sun 8.15am–7.15pm) is home to the greatest collection of Venetian art and is the most-visited spot in the city after Piazza San Marco and the Palazzo Ducale. A maximum of 180 visitors are allowed in at any one time, so arrive early to avoid the queues or make a reservation (tel: 041-520 0345; www.gallerieaccademia.it).

The collection spans paintings from the 14th to the 18th centuries, arranged roughly chronologically in 24 rooms. But be selective and focus on the museum's highlights at least. At the time of writing, the Accademia's first floor was undergoing major renovation with many of its rooms closed until 2020 and some of the artworks not on display. But the good news is that the restored Sala Grande,

Tintoretto's *Transport of St Mark*, Accademia collection

the magnificent confraternity hall, can already be seen in all its glory.

Room 2 contains Carpaccio's striking *Crucifixion of the Ten Thousand Martyrs*, while **Room 4** draws crowds of art lovers for its exquisite paintings, including Mantegna's *St George* and a fine series of works by Giovanni Bellini and Giorgione. **Room 5** holds the most famous work of art in the gallery, Giorgione's moody and enigmatic *Tempest*; it also houses *Portrait of an Old Woman*, by the same artist.

In **Room 10** look out for Veronese's *Feast at the House of Levi*, a painting of a raucous Renaissance banquet originally entitled (and meant to depict) *The Last Supper*. When church officials condemned the work as sacrilegious and ordered Veronese to change it, he blithely did nothing but change its name. Jacopo Tintoretto's dazzling St Mark paintings, notably the haunting *Transport of the Body of St Mark*, are also here, as is Titian's

☑ VENETIAN ARTISTS

Jacopo Bellini (1400–70) and his sons **Giovanni** (1430–1516) and **Gentile** (1429–1507) inaugurated the *Serenissima's* glorious era of art in the 15th century.

The Venetian High Renaissance began with **Giorgione** (c.1477–1510), whose great promise can be seen in *Tempest*, at the Accademia.

Vittore Carpaccio (1445–1526) painted detailed scenes of city life as well as the splendid series on the life of St Ursula at the Accademia.

Titian (1490–1576) was widely hailed as the finest painter of his era. Only a few of his works can be seen in Venice; these include the *Assumption of the Virgin*, above the altar of the Frari church.

Jacopo Tintoretto (1518–94) was a quiet, religious man who left Venice only once. Most of his work remains in the city. See his genius in the Scuola di San Rocco and his parish church of Madonna dell'Orto.

Paolo Veronese (1528–88) is inextricably linked with the church of San Sebastiano, which is resplendent with his paintings. Many of his works are in the Accademia.

Antonio Canaletto (1697–1768) is famed for his detailed paintings of Venice but only three are on show in the city – most were sold abroad by his English patron, Josef Smith.

Perhaps the greatest Venetian decorative painter was **Giovanni Battista Tiepolo** (1696–1770), who covered the ceiling of the upper hall in the Scuola Grande dei Carmini with nine masterly paintings.

dark *Pietà*, the artist's last work, intended for his tomb. **Room 11** contains masterpieces by Veronese and Tintoretto, as well as Tiepolo's *Rape of Europa*, a triumph of pulsating light and shade, while **Room 17** contains a real rarity – the Accademia's only painting by Canaletto.

Out of sequence, **Room 23** is housed in the top of the church that constitutes part of the gallery structure. The airy, spacious loft

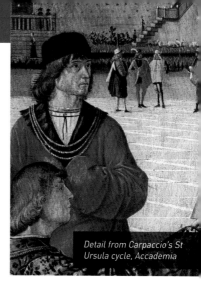

Detail from Carpaccio's St Ursula cycle, Accademia

is the perfect setting for some splendid altarpieces, notably the faded but powerful *Blessed Lorenzo Giustinian* by Gentile Bellini. **Room 20** is probably the most stunning in the Accademia, with four immense paintings occupying one wall apiece. Gentile Bellini's celebrated *Procession around the Piazza Bearing the Cross* reveals how little San Marco has changed since 1496, except for its mosaics and the addition of the Campanile and Procuratie Nuove. Other illustrious paintings include Carpaccio's epic *Miracle of the Holy Cross at the Rialto Bridge*, showing the old bridge at the Rialto and gondolas on the Grand Canal.

In **Room 21** is Carpaccio's lyrical, poetically narrative *St Ursula* cycle, which depicts the tragic life of this Breton heroine. It spans her acceptance of the hand of the British prince, Hereus, on condition of his conversion to Christianity, to their subsequent pilgrimage to Rome and eventual martyrdom at the hands of Attila the Hun.

On the second floor, the **Quadreria** (closed for restoration at the time of writing) is packed with yet more Venetian masterpieces.

COLLEZIONE PEGGY GUGGENHEIM

Just to the east of the Accademia along the Grand Canal, in the Palazzo Venier dei Leoni, is another exceptional museum, the **Collezione Peggy Guggenheim ⓿** (www.guggenheim-venice. it; Wed–Mon 10am–6pm), which is generally regarded as one of the best modern art collections in Europe. The bequest of American expatriate and heiress Peggy Guggenheim, who died in 1979, is displayed in the building she made her home: an eccentrically designed, one-storey 18th-century palace (still unfinished), with its gardens and terrace overlooking the Grand Canal. Guggenheim was renowned for her hospitality, and the museum stages regular events, from late openings to concerts and drinks parties. The welcoming museum café, with a menu designed by the owner of Ai Gondolieri, is also one of the better restaurants in Venice.

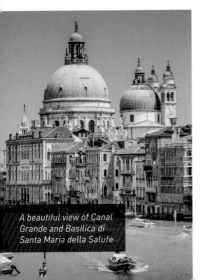
A beautiful view of Canal Grande and Basilica di Santa Maria della Salute

Among the outstanding exhibits are early Picassos and Chagalls and Brancusi's bronze sculpture *Bird in Space*. Other highlights include works by Max Ernst (whom Guggenheim married), Dalí, Miró, Piet Mondrian and Jackson Pollock, as well as a sculpture by Calder that Guggenheim used in lieu of a headboard for her bed. Sculptures by Giacometti dot the garden. Don't miss Marino Marini's *Angel of the Citadel*, a bold, joyfully erotic bronze equestrian statue in the garden facing the Grand Canal.

Henry Moore sculpture at the Collezione Peggy Guggenheim

LA SALUTE

Having presided over the entrance to the Grand Canal for over 300 years, the magnificent baroque church of **Santa Maria della Salute** ⓫ (daily 9am–noon, 3–5.30pm) is almost as familiar a Venetian landmark as the Basilica di San Marco. The church, popularly known among the Venetians as 'La Salute', was built as an offering of thanks to the Virgin Mary for the end of a catastrophic plague in 1630 – the plague wiped out over a third of the lagoon's inhabitants. Under the direction of the young architect, Baldassare Longhena, construction began in 1631 and more than one million oak pilings were sunk into the swampy earth to support the massive structure. Longhena lived to see the church, his life's work, completed in 1682. Each year, on 21 November, the church's feast day (Festa della Salute), engineers build a great pontoon of boats over the Grand Canal, and most of the city's population, resident and visiting, join a procession across the water and into the church. This is the only day that the church's main doors are opened.

Inside, in the sacristy to the left of the high altar, is Tintoretto's magnificent painting of the *Marriage at Cana*. Three Titians (*Cain and Abel*, *Abraham Sacrificing Isaac* and *David and Goliath*) are also on view.

DOGANA

Continue east from the Salute towards the tip of Dorsoduro. At this point you'll find the 17th-century **Dogana da Mar** (Customs House), where the cargoes from all incoming ships were inspected in former days. The long-abandoned building has been converted by Japanese architect, Tadao Ando, into the **Punta della Dogana Contemporary Art Centre** (www.palazzograssi.it; Wed–Mon 10am–7pm which has rotating displays of artworks from the world-class collection of François Pinault, owner of the Palazzo Grassi (see page 77; combined ticket). Designed like a ship's prow, this 17th-century Customs House is crowned by two bronze Atlas figures bearing a golden globe, with the weathervane figure of Fortuna on top. Striking contemporary sculptures also adorn the quaysides, notably the *Boy with Frog* who is perched on the point, and a bold talking point on the Zattere side, part installation, part hoist.

Lap up the views from here, looking straight into the Bacino di San Marco (St Mark's Basin) in one direction and across the **Canale della Giudecca** (Giudecca Canal) in the other. The vista takes in the islands of Giudecca and San Giorgio Maggiore, including three churches designed by Andrea Palladio: the imposing **San Giorgio Maggiore** (see page 78); **Le Zitelle** (the Church of the Spinsters); and the landmark **Redentore** (Redeemer). The last was built, like the Salute after it, as an act of thanksgiving at the end of the devastating plague of 1575–6. As at the Salute,

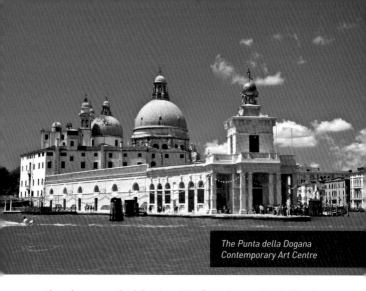

The Punta della Dogana Contemporary Art Centre

there is an annual celebration at the Redentore each third Sunday of July; the festivities culminate in a flotilla of small boats and a spectacular display of fireworks over the water.

ZATTERE

The **Fondamente delle Zattere** (Quay of the Rafts), runs all the way along the southern waterfront from the Dogana to the Rio di San Sebastiano. The floating rafts that gave the Zattere its name were once major unloading points for cargoes of salt. The huge salt warehouse, once capable of storing over 40,000 tons of the mineral, now doubles as an exhibition centre and as a boathouse for a local rowing club.

Continue along the Zattere past the churches of Spirito Santo and the Gesuati (Santa Maria del Rosario). Turn right on to the Fondamenta Nani and you'll see the rustic **Squero di San Trovaso** on the other side (*squero* means boatyard).

Classic gondolier garb

In the 16th century, when thousands of gondolas plied the waters, there were many *squeri*; nowadays, San Trovaso is the only one where you can see gondolas repaired. The church of **San Trovaso** (Mon–Sat 2.30–5.30pm) is worth investigating for two of Tintoretto's last works, both completed by his son.

Head back to the Zattere, which, with its cafés and restaurants, is a good place to take a break. The huge red-brick landmark that you can see across the water right at the western end of Giudecca is the **Molino Stucky**, a flour mill that was part of an attempt to bring modern industry to Venice in the 1890s. Now reborn as the Hilton Molino Stucky, the hotel has ravishing rooftop views, a swimming pool, and Skyline, an exciting rooftop cocktail bar.

GIUDECCA

When you have time, cross over to **Giudecca**, Venice's most diverse neighbourhood, where palatial hotels like the Hilton Molino Stucky are cheek by jowl with authentic inns, a boatyard and earthy working-class bars. Giudecca feels like a thriving community, with arty incomers living beside gondola-makers, boat-repairers, sailors, celebrities and craftspeople. When monumental Venice palls, or the crowds feel overwhelming, just hop on a ferry to Giudecca for an unfussy lunch and views or for sunset wanderings and cocktails.

For now, turn right along the Zattere waterfront and, at the San Basilio landing stage, head inland, following the canal north. Cross the tiny bridge for the splendid 16th-century church of **San Sebastiano** (www.chorusvenezia.org; Mon–Sat 10.30am–4.30pm). It is a tribute to Veronese, who painted most of the opulent works decorating the walls, altar and ceiling from 1555 to 1565. The artist is also buried here.

The next square west is Campo Angelo Raffaele, named after its 17th century church. The adjoining canal leads to the humble parish church of **San Nicolò dei Mendicoli** (Mon–Sat

⊙ GONDOLAS AND GONDOLIERS

Nothing is more quintessentially Venetian than the gondola, although nowadays they are more a tourist attraction than a means of transportation. Gondolas have existed since the 11th century, and in the 18th century around 14,000 plied Venice's canals; today, the number has fallen to 400.

All gondolas are made to the same specifications, built by hand from around 280 separate pieces of wood. Curiously, they are asymmetrical (the left side is wider than the right) in order to accommodate the gondolier as he rows and steers. Gondolas are painted black in deference to the sumptuary laws of 1562 that attempted to curb the extravagances of Venetian society. They also retain a rather curious metallic pronged prow (or *ferro*). Several explanations have been offered for the symbolism and shape of the *ferro*: some think that the blades represent the six districts of Venice; others maintain that the shape suggests the Grand Canal or even the doge's cap.

Many gondoliers still wear the traditional outfit of straw boater, striped T-shirt and white sailor's top.

10am–noon, 3–5.30pm, Sun 9am–noon) – often overlooked, but its modest exterior belies its lavishly decorated interior. The church was founded in the 7th century, making it one of the oldest in the city, and remodelled between the 12th and 14th centuries; it was restored in 1977 by the Venice in Peril Fund. The church's single nave is graced by Romanesque columns, Gothic capitals and beamed ceilings, and adorned by Renaissance panelling, gilded statuary and School of Veronese paintings.

THE UNIVERSITY QUARTER

The attractive area between the Accademia and Campo Santa Margherita is popular with students and younger visitors. In term time **Campo Santa Margherita** ⓬, home to bars, inns, bohemian shops and colourful market stalls, is the liveliest square in Venice outside Piazza San Marco. At one end of the square is the restored church of **Santa Margherita**, while at the other end is the spacious and ornately decorated **Chiesa dei Carmini** (Church of the Carmelites). For even more religious art, call in next door at **I Carmini** (www.scuolagrande carmini.it; daily 11am–5pm), the headquarters of the Scuola Grande dei Carmini and a showcase to Tiepolo, who covered the ceiling of the Upper Hall with nine paintings, the last one completed in 1744.

From Campo Santa Margherita the Rio Terrà street leads southeast towards **Campo San Barnaba** which sits on the other side of San Barnaba canal. Here you'll see an attractive fruit-and-vegetable barge moored along the quay, and the solemn, neoclassical church of **San Barnaba**, which film buffs may recognise as the setting for major scenes in *Summertime* (1955) starring Katharine Hepburn, and *Indiana Jones and the Last Crusade* (1989) with Harrison Ford.

Dining in Campo Santa Margherita Square

CA' REZZONICO

On the other side of the San Barnaba canal where it meets the Grand Canal is the glorious 17th-century **Ca' Rezzonico** ⓫ (www.visitmuve.it; Wed–Mon 10.30am–6pm, Nov–Mar until 4.30pm), home to the **Museo del Settecento Veneziano** (Museum of 18th-Century Venice), another of Dorsoduro's major art collections. Here, however, the 17th-century pala-tial setting is just as important as the 18th-century exhibits it houses.

Stepping into the Ca' Rezzonico is a feast for the eyes. At the top of the vast entrance staircase is a ballroom, featuring two immense Murano-glass chandeliers as well as decorated ceilings and walls. In the adjacent room are intricately carved figures of chained slaves.

Ceilings by Tiepolo (father and son) are the main artistic interest until you reach the gallery on the second floor. Most visitors are drawn to the two Canaletto paintings of the Grand Canal – there are only three paintings by him in the whole of Venice. You'll also find works by Pietro Longhi, who recorded the final, decadent century of the Venetian Republic. On the third and fourth floors of the museum, the Gallery Egidio Martini showcases an impressive collection of around 300 works, mainly by Venetian painters.

The views from the windows overlooking the Grand Canal are also to be savoured. Pen Browning, the son of poet Robert Browning, owned this palace in the late 19th century and his father died here in 1889. The American-born artist James Whistler also lived here from 1879 to 1880.

SAN POLO AND SANTA CROCE

The two adjoining *sestieri* of San Polo and Santa Croce are curved into the left bank of the Grand Canal. Together they are home to many important sights, including the artistic treasure houses of the church of the Frari and the Scuola Grande di San Rocco, as well as one of the city's most vibrant markets, on the Rialto.

THE RIALTO

Not only Venice's oldest district, the **Rialto** is also the area with the greatest concentration of Veneto-Byzantine palaces. From its earliest foundation, this was the powerhouse of the Republic, and a crossroads between the East and the West. On a practical level, it also acted as a busy commercial exchange and meeting place for merchants. As such, it is often described as 'Venice's kitchen, office and back parlour'. During the peak of the Republic's influence it was one of the most important financial centres in Europe.

Ponte di Rialto

The **Ponte di Rialto** (Rialto Bridge) divides the city into two, with the right bank, on the San Marco side, known as the *Rialto di quà* (this side), and the left bank known as the *Rialto di là* (that side). The bridge spans the Grand Canal with a strong, elegantly curved arch of marble, and is lined with shops selling silk ties, scarves, leather and jewellery. Henry James appreciated the 'small shops and booths that abound in Venetian character' but also felt 'the communication of insect life'.

The current bridge is merely the last in a line that began with simple pontoons and then progressed to a wooden structure, with a drawbridge section to allow the passage of tall ships. A new bridge was created in 1588–91 by Antonio da Ponte following the collapse of the previous one. Tradition has it that the greatest architects of the day, including Michelangelo and Palladio, competed for the commission, but da Ponte's design was chosen.

The result is a light, floating structure with shops nestling in its solid, closed arches. From the bridge one can admire the majestic sweep of palaces and warehouses swinging away to La Volta del Canal, the great elbow-like bend in the Grand Canal.

The Rialto markets

The **Rialto markets** ⑮ make a refreshing change from the monumental Venice of San Marco. Ignore the tourist tat in favour of foodstuffs galore – and forays to traditional or contemporary *bacari* (Venetian wine and tapas bars). These serve anything from sushi to asparagus parcels or baby artichokes, salt cod or meatballs.

The **Erberia** is a fruit-and-vegetable market overlooking the Grand Canal. Casanova relished its 'innocent pleasure', but latter-day foodies find pleasure in the profusion of herbs, flowers, fruit, Veneto wines and vegetables.

The markets extend along the bank to the **Pescheria**, the fish market, set in an arcaded neo-Gothic hall by the quayside, a design inspired by Carpaccio's realistic paintings. Under the porticoes, fishermen display their catch on mountains of ice. The adjoining **Campo delle Beccarie**, once a public abattoir, now contains market overspill and lively foodie bars.

CAMPO SAN POLO

The biggest square in the city outside Piazza San Marco, **Campo San Polo** is notable for its church and for the mid-14th-century rose-coloured **Palazzo Soranzo**, situated just opposite. Casanova came to this palace in the 18th century as a young, hired violinist, living as the adopted son and heir to the family fortune with an entrée to Venetian society. From here, he went on to seduce and outrage Europe's 18th-century aristocracy.

Note the fine portal of the church of **San Polo** ⑯ (www.cho rusvenezia.org; Mon–Sat 10.30am–4.30pm), one of the few features that survives from the original 15th-century building. The interior, reached through a side door, features a brooding *Last Supper* by Tintoretto and Giandomenico Tiepolo's *Via Crucis (Stations of the Cross)* painted when he was only 20 years old. A campanile, dating from 1362, stands a short way from the church and is adorned with two of the Republic's less-appealing lions, one playing with a human head, the other with a serpent.

THE FRARI

Santa Maria Gloriosa dei Frari ⑰ (known simply as the Frari, a deformation of *frati*, meaning 'brothers'; www.chorusvenezia. org; Mon–Sat 9am–6pm, Sun 1–6pm) is Venice's second church after San Marco and the resting place of the painter Titian.

The Frari is Venice's largest Gothic church

The brothers in question – members of the Franciscan order – were granted a piece of land in 1236, and the church, a huge lofty structure, was rebuilt between 1340 and 1469.

The church's greatest treasure is the soaring, mysterious *Assumption* (1518) hanging in the Gothic apse above the high altar. One of Titian's early masterpieces, this painting helped to establish his reputation. To the right is Donatello's much-admired wooden statue of *St John the Baptist*. Restored during the 19th century, it is the Florentine artist's sole remaining work in Venice. Tucked away in the sacristy on the right is the *Madonna and Saints* (1488), a triptych by Giovanni Bellini. Don't miss the beautiful marquetry and intricate carving on the choir stalls – this choir is one of the few in Venetian churches to stand in its original location.

The Frari is also notable for its huge monuments to Titian and to the 19th-century sculptor, Canova, on opposite sides of the great nave. Although Titian was buried here in 1576, the monument to him was not built until the mid-19th century. Canova's mausoleum was erected in 1827, five years after his death; however, only his heart is interred here.

Several doges are entombed in the Frari, including two in the high altar. The church is also home to one of the city's most bombastic monuments, which is dedicated to Doge Giovanni Pesaro and situated next to Canova's mausoleum.

Titian's wife

Before you leave the Frari church, be sure to note the splendid *Madonna di Ca' Pesaro* by Titian, which is thought to represent the artist's wife.

SCUOLA GRANDE DI SAN ROCCO

The nearby **Scuola Grande di San Rocco** ⓲ (www.scuolagrandesanrocco.it; daily 9.30am–5.30pm) stirs the

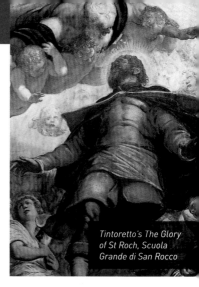

Tintoretto's The Glory of St Roch, Scuola Grande di San Rocco

emotions. John Ruskin, the foremost Venetian art historian of the 19th century and one of the city's most scrupulous observers, described San Rocco as having one of the three most precious picture collections in all of Italy. The novelist Henry James was also a devotee, although he found the Scuola Grande a little too breathtaking, proclaiming it to be 'suffocating'.

In 1564 Tintoretto won a competition to decorate the interior, and for the next 23 years much of his time was spent painting the 65 pictures here. The artist began upstairs in the sumptuous **Sala dell'Albergo**, just off the main hall, so make your way straight there before coming back down to the lower hall. On the ceiling is Tintoretto's *The Glory of St Roch*, which was the work that won him the commission. His monumental *Crucifixion* in the same room is said to have been considered by the artist to be his greatest painting.

In the dimly lit main hall, the gilded **ceiling** is covered with 21 immense pictures, and there are another 13 on the walls (all of which are captioned on the helpful plan provided free at the entrance). The best way of studying the ceiling works is to focus on the detail, rather than attempting to take in broad sweeps at once. Hidden in the gloom below the murals are some wonderful, if slightly odd, wooden figures by Venice's offbeat 17th-century sculptor Francesco Pianto.

In contrast to the pictures in the main hall, those on the ground floor (representing scenes from the life of the Virgin) seem almost playful. Look out for *The Flight into Egypt*, widely acknowledged as another of Tintoretto's great paintings. More Tintorettos are on display in the church of San Rocco next door.

CASA DI CARLO GOLDONI

Close to Campo San Polo and the Frari is the **Casa di Carlo Goldoni** (www.visitmuve.it; Thu–Tue noon–5pm), the house in which the playwright Carlo Goldoni was born in 1707. In 1952 the house was turned into a small museum dedicated to the writer and his works, and although the contents are quite specialist, the house is worth a visit for its well-preserved Gothic architecture, especially its handsome courtyard.

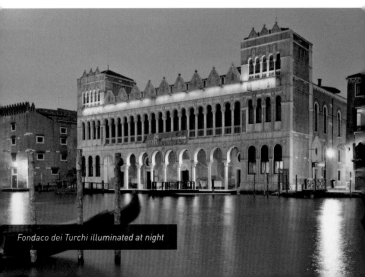

Fondaco dei Turchi illuminated at night

FONDACO DEI TURCHI

The main route north from Campo di San Polo brings you into the large, rambling Campo San Giacomo dell'Orio. From here follow the Calle Larga and Fondamenta del Megio for the **Fondaco dei Turchi** ⑲, built in 1227 as a warehouse and meeting place for merchants, but now home to the **Museo di Storia Naturale** (Natural History Museum; www.visitmuve.

The Meeting Between Titian (1488-1576) and young Veronese (1528-88)

it; June–Oct Tue–Fri 10am–6pm, Sat–Sun 10.30am–6pm, Nov–May Tue–Fri 9am–5pm, Sat–Sun 10.30am–5pm). This is a rather old-fashioned collection, but still popular with children.

Among the more terrifying exhibits are a monster crab with legs 2m (6.5ft) long and a scorpion over 30cm (1ft) long. The most impressive exhibits, however, are in the dinosaur room, notably the bones of possibly the largest extinct crocodilian creatures ever found (11m/37ft in length) and the complete skeleton of a massive biped reptile known as an *ouranosaurus* (almost 3.5m/12ft high and some 7m/23ft long).

CA' PESARO

Zigzag your way east for the next museum on the Grand Canal, the **Galleria Internazionale d'Arte Moderna**, beyond the San Stae landing stage (www.visitmuve.it; Tue–Sun Apr–Oct

10.30am–6pm, Nov–Mar 10.30am–4.30pm), housed in the baroque **Ca' Pesaro 20**. The gallery was founded with the best of the Biennale exhibition pieces and features mainly Italian artists, with a few important international contemporary works.

Upstairs in the same building is the **Museo d'Arte Orientale** (same opening times as Ca' Pesaro and combined ticket), a rather confusing jumble of lacquered pieces, Samurai arms and armour and other artefacts given to Venice by Austria after World War I as reparation for bombing attacks on the city.

CANNAREGIO

This district, close to the railway station, is the most northerly one in Venice. Its name comes from *canne*, meaning reeds, indi-

Fondamenta Madonna dell'Orto

cating its marshy origins. This is an ancient quarter, often scorned by the snobbish in favour of the more stylish Dorsoduro – ironically, this was once a fashionable spot, dotted with foreign embassies and palatial gardens. The palaces may be faded, but Cannaregio remains both a retreat for cognoscenti and the last bastion for working-class Venetians who have not moved to the Mestre mainland. It is also the site of the world's first Jewish ghetto.

THE GHETTO

For almost 300 years, until Napoleon ended the practice in 1797, the Jews of Venice were permitted to live only in this tiny section of Cannaregio, surrounded on all sides by canals. The area had previously been a foundry or *ghetto* in Venetian; the word *'ghetto'* subsequently came to denote Jewish and other segregated quarters all over the world.

Star of David in the Ghetto

Jewish refugees fleeing the War of Cambrai in 1508 came in their thousands to settle here. At the Ghetto's peak in the 17th century, its inhabitants numbered some 5,000, and the limited space led to the building of tenements six storeys high (still tall for Venice). Venetian Jews were severely taxed, forced to wear distinctive clothing, barred from many professions and made to observe a curfew, which was strictly enforced by watchmen.

However, by the 16th century, the Ghetto was flourishing, with choirs and literary salons that were visited by non-Jewish Venetians. The market at the Campo del Ghetto was the lively 'pawnshop of Venice' – an international attraction where treasures from the great houses of Venice's recently bankrupt or dead were bought and sold.

Today, the Ghetto is a quiet residential corner of Venice, with only a small Jewish population, though the area is rich in Jewish culture with restaurants, bakeries and shops

A gilded gondola

selling Jewish handicrafts. The revamped and expanded
Museo Ebraico ㉑ (Jewish Museum; www.museoebraico.it;
Sun–Fri June–Sept 10am–7pm, Oct–May until 5.30pm) located
in the Campo del Ghetto Nuovo, contains a remarkable collection of Italian Judaica and runs tours of synagogues in the area
every hour from 10.30am–5.30pm, in winter until 4.30pm. On
the opposite side of the square, a series of reliefs commemo-
rates the 202 Venetian Jews who died in World War II.

MADONNA DELL'ORTO

The 15th-century church of the **Madonna dell'Orto** ㉒ (Our
Lady of the Garden; www.madonnadellorto.org; Mon–Sat
10am–5pm, Sun noon–5pm) occupies a quiet spot northeast
of the Ghetto. After crossing the canal north of the Campo di
Ghetto Nuovo, follow the bank east before turning left onto
Calle Larga and continuing north through the Campo dei Mori.

The church, which has a delicate Gothic facade and lovely cloister, was built to house a miraculous statue of the Virgin and Child, found in a nearby garden (orto). However, it is best known nowadays for its connections with the Renaissance painter Tintoretto – this was his parish church, and he is buried with his family to the right of the choir, near the high altar. The church is filled with Tintoretto's paintings, including his *Last Judgement*, *The Worship of the Golden Calf* and the *Presentation of the Virgin* (over the sacristy door), which demonstrates the artist's theatricality and grandiosity. Also of interest is Cima da Conegliano's remarkable painting of *St John the Baptist*, to the right of the entrance.

CA' D'ORO

Head south from the Madonna dell'Orto towards the Strada Nova, which leads east to the **Ca' d'Oro** ㉓, the finest Venetian Gothic palace in the city, which is best viewed from the Grand Canal. Inside is the **Galleria Franchetti** (www.cadoro.org; Mon 9am–2pm, Tue–Sun 9am–7pm), home to Mantegna's gruesome *St Sebastian*, depicting the saint riddled with arrows, some notable Renaissance sculpture, minor paintings by Tintoretto and Titian, and remnants of frescoes recovered from other buildings, including some by Giorgione.

BOAT TRIP ALONG THE GRAND CANAL

The extraordinary main artery through Venice, the **Grand Canal** (Canal Grande) – or *Canalazzo*, as it is known to the locals – stretches over 4km (2 miles), from inauspicious

The 'little dyer'

Tintoretto (1518–94), who spent his whole life in Venice, was nicknamed after his father's trade as a dyer.

beginnings near the Stazione Ferrovia (railway station) to a glorious final outpouring into the Basino di San Marco (St Mark's Basin). The views along the canal are so wonderful that many visitors ride the *vaporetti* back and forth for hours, soaking up the atmosphere; a good waterbus to take is the inappropriately named *accelerato* (No. 1), which stops at every landing stage.

The banks of the canal are lined with more than 200 ornate palaces and grand houses, most built between the 14th and 18th centuries. While some have been superbly restored, others have a neglected air, awaiting their turn for renovation. Very few of these homes are still inhabited by the aristocratic families for whom they were built; the majority have been turned into offices, hotels, apartments or gallery spaces.

The following section details some of the most outstanding palaces to look for while travelling along the canal from the railway station (Stazione Ferrovia) towards Piazza San Marco.

FONDACO DEI TURCHI TO THE CA' D'ORO

The first building of note on the right bank is the **Fondaco dei Turchi**, which is home to the Natural History Museum. Built in Veneto-Byzantine style in 1227 (though brutally restored in the 19th century), it is one of the Grand Canal's oldest survivors,

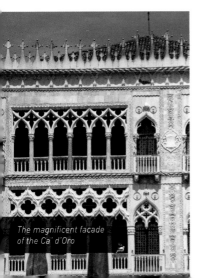

The magnificent facade of the Ca' d'Oro

once a trading base and living quarters for Turkish merchants.

Just beyond the San Marcuola landing stage on the left bank is the **Palazzo Vendramin-Calergi**, (www.vendramincalergi.com) designed by Mauro Coducci (1440–1504). The German composer Richard Wagner died here in 1883 and his apartments are open to visitors Tuesday and Saturday mornings and Thursday afternoons (booking required, tel: 041-276 0407 or 338-416 4174; www.casinovenezia.it/en/wagner-museum); the building also provides an opulent setting for Venice's Casino (www.casinovenezia.it).

Ponte di Calatrava

The Calatrava Bridge, a controversial fourth bridge over the Grand Canal, links Piazzale Roma with the railway station, and is named after its Spanish architect, Santiago Calatrava. While visitors often love its sinuous design, many Venetians see the exciting glass and steel structure as incongruous and superfluous. The issue of access for the disabled has also yet to be fully resolved. Further controversy is expected over the renovation of the Rialto and Academia bridges.

Beyond the San Stae stop on the right bank is the vast baroque **Ca' Pesaro**, designed by Baldassare Longhena (the architect of the Salute). Decorated with grotesque masks, the Ca' (short for *Casa*, or house) was completed in 1682 and is now home to two art museums.

By the next landing stage is the **Ca' d'Oro** (home to the Galleria Franchetti), built in the first quarter of the 15th century for the wealthy patrician Marino Contarini. The Ca' was originally covered in gold leaf, hence its name, which means 'House of Gold'. It is one of the most famous frontages on the Grand Canal, renowned for its elaborate Gothic facade decorated with magnificent tracery.

PAST THE RIALTO

Just north of the Rialto, on the left bank, stands the 13th-century Veneto-Byzantine-style **Ca' da Mosto**, one of the oldest houses on the canal. Nearby is the landmark **Ponte di Rialto** (Rialto Bridge). Also on the left bank, to the south, are the handsome twin 13th-century *palazzi* **Loredan** and **Farsetti**, which now function as the town hall. After the San Silvestro stop, on the right bank is the splendid mid-13th century **Palazzo Bernardo**, which may look familiar, since its tracery mirrors that of the Palazzo Ducale.

AROUND THE BEND

Opposite the San Tomà stop is the **Palazzo Mocenigo** complex, marked by blue-and-white mooring posts *(pali)*. The poet Lord Byron lived here from 1819 to 1824, while balancing the needs of a number of fiery local mistresses and working on his mock-heroic narrative poem *Don Juan*. Byron's most daring Venetian venture was to swim in a race against two other men from the Lido all the way to the Rialto – an excellent swimmer, the poet was the only one to finish. Today, the Grand Canal is no longer clean enough for such aquatic feats.

On the bend of the canal, on the opposite side, look out for three attractive palaces: the **Balbi** (1590), the restored **Ca' Foscari** (1437), home to the university, and finally the

Giustinian (c.1452), where Wagner composed part of his opera *Tristan and Isolde*.

Located a few blocks on is the glorious 17th-century **Ca' Rezzonico**, home to the Museo del Settecento Veneziano. Opposite is the 18th-century **Palazzo Grassi** (www.palazzograssi.it; Wed–Mon 10am–7pm) which belongs to the French magnate, François Pinault, and houses his magnificent collection of contemporary art, as does the Punta della Dogana. The palace can only accommodate a fraction of the vast collection; it is also used as a venue for blockbuster art exhibitions.

PONTE DELL'ACCADEMIA TO LA SALUTE

A little further on, the soon-to-be-restored **Ponte dell'Accademia** (Accademia Bridge) was built as a temporary wooden arch in 1932, replacing an iron structure erected by the Austrians that had become an obstruction to larger *vaporetti*. The bridge has fine views towards La Salute.

The splendid building to the left, with the classic red-and-white *pali*, is the 15th-century **Palazzo Cavalli Franchetti**, while the neighbouring **Palazzo Barbaro**, built from the 15th to the 17th centuries, was much favoured by the artistic and literary set – writers Robert Browning and Henry James, and artists John Singer Sargent, Claude Monet and James Whistler all spent time here.

Next en route is the right bank's **Palazzo Barbarigo**, decorated with strikingly gaudy, late-19th-century mosaics. Close by, the one-storey **Palazzo Venier dei Leoni** is home to the Collezione Peggy Guggenheim. The final building to note as you head along the canal towards its mouth is the gently listing 15th-century **Ca' Dario** (or Palazzo Dario). Five centuries of scandal, from suicides to bankruptcy to suspicious deaths, have plagued the house. Note its funnel-shaped chimney pots, designed to reduce the risk of fire.

THE ISLANDS

A highlight of any visit to Venice is a *vaporetto* trip through the inviting lagoon. Although many of its small islands are uninhabited wildernesses, inaccessible by public transport, there is a range of others to visit, from glass-making Murano to colourful Burano and serene Torcello. Here are some suggestions for leisurely half-day or one-day island excursions (for Giudecca, see page 58).

SAN GIORGIO MAGGIORE

San Giorgio Maggiore ㉔ is the closest island to the city, located almost within swimming distance of the Palazzo Ducale. The only major island that is untouched by commerce, it is home to a magnificent Palladian monastic complex and is celebrated for glorious views back over the lagoon towards Venice. To reach the island, take the No. 2 *vaporetto*; the journey lasts little more than 5 minutes.

Palladio's church (www.abbaziasangiorgio.it; daily 9am–7pm, 8.30am–6pm in winter) was completed in 1610, and the

⊙ REST IN PEACE?

Nowhere is Venice's chronic lack of available land brought home so vividly as on the cemetery island of San Michele. In the early 1800s Napoleon decreed that burials should no longer take place in the city, and on San Michele they are not so much welcomed as tolerated. Burial lasts for 10 years only, however, and unless the deceased has made provision for an extension on his or her lease – something that few Venetians can afford – then at the end of that time the remains are exhumed and sent to an ossuary to make way for the next occupant.

result is a masterpiece of proportion and harmonious space. Tintoretto's *Last Supper* and *The Gathering of Manna* (both 1592–4) grace either side of the chancel. The high altar is dominated by a large bronze group by Girolamo Campagna and represents the evangelists sustaining the world. Behind are the church's splendidly carved 16th-century choir stalls.

San Giorgio Maggiore

For most visitors, however, the church takes second place to the view from its 200-year-old campanile. Take the lift to the top for one of the great panoramas of Venice, then look down into the cloister of the **monastery** below to see a rare grassy space. The Fondazione Cini museum and glass centre (www.cini.it) occupies much of the monastic complex. Guided tours take place hourly daily (mid-Mar–mid-Dec 10am–6pm), covering the library, refectory, cloisters and Teatro Verde, the open-air theatre.

SAN MICHELE

The island of **San Michele** ㉕ is the site of the city's cemetery, hence its sombre nickname, the 'island of the dead'. It lies 400m/yds from Fondamenta Nuove and is accessed by *vaporetti* Nos 4.1 and 4.2, which stop right outside **San Michele in Isola**, an elegant Renaissance church clad in glistening white Istrian stone.

Contemporary Murano glass

Go through the cloister to reach the **cemetery** (daily Apr–Sept 7.30am–6pm, Oct–Mar 7.30am–4pm). Among the cypress trees, you can visit the graves of American poet Ezra Pound (1885–1972), in section XV, and composer Igor Stravinsky (1882–1971) and impresario Serge Diaghilev (1872–1929), in section XIV.

MURANO

After San Michele, the *vaporetti* stop at **Murano** ㉖, an island famed for its glassblowing tradition. Free water taxi excursions are offered by glass factories, but if you want to avoid high-pressure sales tactics, take the *vaporetto* and make your own way around the factories instead. Orientation in Murano is a simple matter. From the main quay, where you disembark at the Colonna *vaporetto* stop, stroll along the picturesque Fondamenta dei Vetrai, which leads to Murano's very own Grand Canal.

Although glass was manufactured in Venice as far back as the 10th century, the open furnaces presented such a fire hazard that c.1292 the Republic ordered the factories to be transferred to Murano. Grouped here, the glassblowers kept the secrets of their trade for centuries; the manufacture of mirrors, for instance, was for a long time exclusive to Venice.

The island prospered, and by the early 16th century its population reached some 30,000. Glass artisans were considered honoured citizens. Murano's crystalware decorated royal palaces abroad, and its sumptuous villas housed the leading nobles and diplomats of the city. In time, as other countries learned and applied the secrets of Murano's glassmaking, the island's importance declined, and by the 19th century most of its grand summer residences were no more. However, the glass industry was revived later that century and continues today, though not always up to the old standards and often at over-inflated prices. However, a number of contemporary glass workshops still create outstanding designs.

Signs indicate the **Museo del Vetro** (Glass Museum, Fondamenta Giustinian 8; www.visitmuve.it; daily 10.30am–6pm, Nov–Mar until 4.30pm), containing an eclectic collection of Venetian glass in a 15th-century palazzo. Nearby, on Campo San Donato, is the church of **Santi Maria e Donato** (www.sandonatomurano.it; Mon–Sat 9am–6pm, Sun 12.30–6pm), which is possibly the oldest church in Venice – its 7th-century foundations may predate

Clear vision

It is thought that the Muranesi were the first to invent spectacles, in the early 14th century. By that time they were renowned for their windowpanes, which were the largest and clearest in Europe.

the Basilica di San Marco. The church is splendidly atmospheric, and both the brightly coloured 12th-century mosaic floor and a golden mosaic of the Madonna over the high altar have been sympathetically restored. While you're in the church, note the giant bones behind the altar; these are said to be those of a dragon slain by St Donato. Unlike St George, Donato eschewed the conventional lance and sword, slaying the beast simply by spitting at it.

BURANO

The No. 12 *vaporetto* to **Burano** ➋➐ leaves roughly every half hour from Venice's Fondamenta Nuove; those visiting from Murano can pick the ferry up at the Faro (lighthouse) stop. The journey to Burano and the neighbouring island of Torcello takes around 45 minutes.

Burano is a splash of colour in a bleak lagoon, dispelling any mournfulness with its parade of colourful fishermen's cottages and bobbing boats. Naturally hospitable, the islanders are increasingly known for their "slow food" inns rather than for their lacemaking and fishing traditions.

The island once produced the world's finest lace, and its exquisitely light *punto* in aria pattern was the most sought after in Europe. Nowadays, the lace you see in local shops is largely imported from Asia. But to see authentic Burano lace and the ladies who make it, visit the **Museo del Merletto** (Lace Museum; Piazza Galuppi; www.visitmuve.it; Tue–Sun 10.30am–5pm, Nov–Mar until 4.30pm). Here priceless antique pieces are displayed behind glass, and you can see the Buranesi hunched over their handiwork, valiantly keeping the tradition alive. The school was opened in 1872 to retrain the island's women at a time when the numbers of skilled lacemakers had dwindled to just one.

Burano waterfront

Before leaving the square, visit the 16th-century church of **San Martino** (daily 8am–noon, 3–6pm; free), famous for its 18th-century leaning campanile. San Martino is also home to Tiepolo's *Crucifixion*. Nearby is Da Romano (Via Galuppi 221; www.daromano.it) a hearty fish restaurant that is an art attraction in its own right, its walls are filled with numerous paintings.

SAN FRANCESCO DEL DESERTO

From Burano, the peaceful island of **San Francesco del Deserto** makes a lovely detour. The trip takes about 20 minutes and can normally be arranged with a boatman on Burano's main square. St Francis is said to have landed on the island in 1220, on his return from the Holy Land, and Franciscan friars have been here almost ever since. A handful of the brethren choose to make this a permanent home, while young novices spend a year here as part of their training. The monastery (Tue–Sun 9–11am, 3–5pm) has beautiful 14th-century cloisters and gardens.

TORCELLO

From Burano it's a mere 5-minute hop on the No. 9 *vaporetto* to the remote and evocative island of **Torcello** ㉘. Amazing as it seems now, in early medieval times this overgrown, almost deserted island was the lagoon's principal city, with an estimated population of 20,000. However, with the silting up of its canals into marshes, a consequent outbreak of malaria and then the ascendancy of Venice, there was a mass exodus from the island. Today, there are only about 17 inhabitants on Torcello.

As you walk from the *vaporetto* stop to the cathedral, the canal is the only familiarly Venetian feature. On Torcello, buildings have given way to trees, fields and thick undergrowth. The novelist George Sand captured the pastoral mood in the 1830s, 'Torcello is a reclaimed wilderness. Through copses of water willow and hibiscus bushes run saltwater streams where petrel and teal delight to stalk.'

The solitary path leads past the ancient **Ponte del Diavolo** to a small square where Torcello's cathedral, the church of Santa Fosca and the Museo di Torcello (Torcello Museum) all stand. The Italian-Byzantine cathedral **Santa Maria dell'Assunta** (daily 10.30am–6pm, Nov–Feb 10am–5pm) was founded in 639, but dates mostly from 1008, and is therefore the oldest monument in the lagoon. Among the cathedral's treasures is its original 7th-century altar and a Roman sarcophagus containing the relics of St Heliodorus, first Bishop of Altinum (where the island's first settlers were originally from).

Also among the cathedral's highlights are its rich **mosaics**, judged by many to be the finest in Italy outside those at

Ravenna. A masterpiece of Byzantine design adorns the central apse: a slender, mysterious *Madonna* bathed in a cloth of gold. At the opposite end of the building, an entire wall is covered by a complex, heavily restored *Last Judgement*, probably begun early in the 12th century. The steep climb up the campanile will reward you with a panoramic view of the lagoon.

Santa Fosca (Mon–Sat 10am–6pm, Sun 9am–6pm; free), built in the 11th and 12th centuries and harmoniously combining Romanesque and Byzantine elements, has a bare simplicity rarely found in Venetian churches, while the **Museo di Torcello** (http://museotorcello.servizimetropolitani.ve.it; Tue–Sun 10.30am–5.30pm, Nov–Feb until 5pm) houses a collection salvaged from long-disappeared churches. Outside is a primitive stone chair, known as 'Attila's Throne'; it is possibly an early judge's seat.

THE LIDO

The long strip of land, sandwiched between the city of Venice and the waters of the Adriatic, belongs neither to Venice nor the mainland. This reflects the prime function of the **Lido** 29 to protect Venice from the engulfing tides. In spirit, it is a place apart, not quite a traditional summer resort nor a residential suburb. After the time warp of historic Venice, the sight of cars, villas and department stores can be disconcerting. Yet there is a touch of unreality about the Lido, hence its frequent role as a film set. In this faded fantasy, neo-Gothic piles vie with Art Nouveau villas and a mock-Moorish castle.

Since the Lido cannot compete with the historical riches of the rest of Venice, it generally remains the preserve of residents and visitors staying on the island. Although most day-trippers stray no further than the smart hotels and the beaches where the poets Byron and Shelley once raced on horseback, the Lido offers subtle pleasures for those willing to look, from belle époque architecture to a delightful cycle ride along the sea walls to Malamocco.

The ferries from San Marco deposit visitors among the traffic at the edge of the shopping district. Close to the jetties stands the 16th-century church of **Santa Maria Elisabetta**, behind is the main street, Gran Viale Santa Maria Elisabetta, which cuts across the island from the lagoon shore to the Adriatic. At the far end of the Viale lies the **Lungomare**, the seafront promenade which comes to life during the summer evening *passeggiata* (promenade). Beyond are the best Adriatic beaches, private pockets of sand bedecked with colourful cabins.

The Lido is home to several of the city's most elegant hotels, even if the palatial **Grand Hôtel des Bains** (www.historichotelsthenand now.com/bainsvenicelido.html) of *Death in Venice* fame (see box) is being transformed into chic apartments and a boutique hotel.

⊙ DEATH IN VENICE

Death and Venice go together, with the lagoon a familiar backdrop to modern murder mysteries. The city's taste for the macabre is partly a romanticised notion fed by visions of sinister alleys, the inkiness of a lagoon night or a *cortège* of mourning gondolas gliding across the water. However, Venetian history does provide tales of murdered doges and deadly plots nipped in the bud by the secret police.

And the most celebrated work of literature set in Venice, Thomas Mann's novella *Death in Venice*, does little to dispel the myth. The book follows the decline of the writer Gustav von Aschenbach – a man who believes that art is produced only in 'defiant despite' of corrupting passions and physical weakness. On a reluctant break from work, Aschenbach finds himself in Venice, which Mann depicts as a place of decadence and spiritual dislocation. Aschenbach's obsession with a beautiful Polish boy staying at his hotel (the Lido's former Grand Hôtel des Bains) has dire consequences, as he becomes a slave to his passions, ignoring a cholera epidemic that the corrupt Venetian authorities try to conceal.

Murano glass artwork on display

WHAT TO DO

ENTERTAINMENT

Whenever you go to Venice there will be waterfront cafés made for lingering, Baroque concerts in grand churches, and tiny *bacari* (wine bars) made for toasting the city over a Prosecco and a plate of seafood tapas. Venice offers year-round classical concerts, opera, theatre, art exhibitions and festivals ranging from Carnival to water pageants. These pageants are the glory of Venice, with palaces on the Grand Canal festooned with streamers and silks, redolent of the pomp and pageantry of the Republic.

THE PERFORMING ARTS

Classical music is staged everywhere, but especially in churches and palaces. Popular venues for concerts, from organ recitals to choral works, are the churches of Santo Stefano, the Frari, San Vidal and the Salute. The lavishly decorated Scuole, the charitable confraternities, also stage regular concerts. Baroque music predominates, with the works of former Venice resident Antonio Vivaldi particularly celebrated. The chamber group **Interpreti Veneziani** (www.interpretiveneziani.com) is a good name to look out for – they perform on 18th-century instruments in Chiesa San Vidal (Accademia *vaporetto* stop). Other more operatic ensembles include **Musica a Palazzo** (tel: 971-7272; www.musicapalazzo.com) who perform in a Grand Canal palazzo. In Palazzo Barbarigo-Minotto arias by Verdi and Rossini ring out under a Tiepolo-frescoed ceiling.

Opera in Venice has a rather tragic history – **La Fenice** (The Phoenix), on Campo San Fantin, once dubbed 'the prettiest

Model Alessandra Ambrosio attends the Venice Film Festival

theatre in Europe', was badly damaged by fire in 1996 – its third fire since its construction in 1774. It reopened in 2004 with a triumphant performance of Verdi's *La Traviata*. The opera season runs from November until May (book through www. teatrolafenice.it or www.veneziaunica.it). Opera fans will be tempted by a foray to the summer opera festival in the **Arena** in nearby Verona.

VENICE FILM FESTIVAL

As a major event on the international cinema circuit, the ten-day festival opened in 1932, predating Cannes by 14 years. Founded as a showcase for Fascist Italy, the festival's success belies its unpromising origins. Held in balmy September, Venice welcomes the stars, who can be seen parading along the Lido seafront or sipping Bellinis near St Mark's. To attend, check www.labiennale.org.

NIGHTLIFE

A conservative spirit and an ageing population mean that sleepy Venetian nightlife plays on romance, intimacy and charm rather than cutting-edge clubs and urban thrills. For smart nightlife, call into the cocktail bars in the historic hotels and lap up the stylish San Marco haunts. At the less formal end of the scale, don't leave without popping into one of the city's traditional wine bars, known as *bacari*. Having *cichetti e l'ombra*, a snack and a glass of wine, is a Venetian tradition, similar to Spanish tapas.

Rialto inns

Venice was born as a bazaar city, with the mercantile Rialto at its heart. Latter-day merchants of Venice can still be encountered on a Rialto bar crawl. The canalside Erberia area has become the new meeting place at cocktail hour. These bars

☉ THE COCKTAIL HOUR

Between 6pm and 8pm is 'cocktail time', a Venetian ritual. The locals can be seen sipping wine or classic cocktails in both chic cafés and old-fashioned neighbourhood *bacari*. To look like a Venetian, try the lurid orange cocktail known as *spritz* (pronounced 'spriss' in Venetian dialect). The bright-orange drink was introduced under Austrian rule (named after the introduction of 'selzer', fizzy soda water) and soon became a firm favourite. It consists of roughly equal parts of Prosecco, soda water and Campari or Aperol, garnished with a twist of lemon or an olive. Ask for a *spritz al bitter* for a stronger, less cloying taste. The *spritz* can be an acquired taste, but once acquired, it's the clearest sign that you've fallen for Venice.

tend to be new-wave *bacari* (wine bars) that look traditional but have dared to redesign the menu in tune with the times. Here, you will find **Muro, Naranzaria** and **Bancogiro** – which all feel contemporary yet faithful to the spirit of the old Rialto. Around the corner, the boisterous **Cantina Do Mori** (Calle San Polo 429) has operated since 1462 so it is not inconceivable that Tintoretto was a patron. The artist would have approved of such mixing with the populace, and eating *crostini* with salt cod or a paste of chicken liver and capers.

Cannaregio bars

This bar crawl continues into bohemian Cannaregio, with **Taverna al Campiello Remer** (www.alremer.it) offering a Grand Canal view and tapas in a vaulted inn or come back later for live music. Closer to the Ca d'Oro ferry stop, **Alla Vedova** (Ramo Ca d'Oro, tel: 041-528 5324) is an old-world, cheap-and-cheerful *bacaro*. After fuelling yourself on authentic *cichetti*, call into the neighbouring 'Holy Drinker,' **Il Santo Bevitore** (Cannaregio 2393/A; www.ilsantobevitorepub.com), a canalside corner awash with fans of Trappist ales. If you prefer moody lagoon views, then traipse to **Algiubagio** on the Fondamenta Nuove quaysides (tel: 041-523 6084, see page 109). From the *bacaro* terrace let your eyes feast on San Michele cemetery island while you graze on creative *cichetti*. If the Cannaregio quaysides are a touch bleak, restore your spirits in **Paradiso Perduto** (Fondamenta della Misericordia, tel: 041-720 581), a bohemian live music haunt on a sleepy canalside that wakes up at night.

SHOPPING

The full range of Italian designer goods are on sale in Venice, with designer boutiques clustered around Calle Vallaresso,

Salizzada San Moisè, the Frezzeria and Calle Larga XXII Marzo, west of San Marco. The classic haberdashery quarter is the Mercerie, a maze of alleys sandwiched between San Marco and the Rialto. But above all, seek out traditional Venetian crafts, from stationery to ceramics – including Murano glass and masks only where the provenance is guaranteed. Craft shopping is an intimate experience, a secret glimpse of Venetians at their best.

Luxury shopping in the Dolce & Gabbana shop

CRAFTS, MASKS AND COSTUMES

Atelier Nicolao (Cannaregio 2590, tel: 041-520 7051; www.nico lao.com) is a superb theatrical costumier's. Here you can rent a stunning Carnival disguise and slip back into Casanova's era.

Gianni Basso (Calle del Fumo, Cannaregio 5306, tel: 041-523 4681) supplies personalised stationery that appeals to celebrities and royals.

Paolo Olbi (Dorsoduro 3253, tel: 041-523 7655; http://olbi. atspace.com) is an old-fashioned bookbinder producing gorgeous hand-tooled, leatherbound notebooks.

Papier Mâché (Calle Lunga Santa Maria Formosa, Castello 5174, tel: 041-522 9995) is an authentic mask shop run by Stefano Gottardo, who helped relaunch Carnival and mask-making.

Masked Art (http://maskedart.myshopify.com) is an online shop selling masks made by legendary Guerrino Lovato, known as the 'king of masks' in Venice.

GLASSWARE

It's fashionable to mock Murano glass, but the best pieces are works of art, from show-stopping chandeliers to sophisticated sculptures signed by great Italian artists and designers. The illustrious names include Barovier & Toso (Fondamenta Vetrai 28, Murano, tel: 041-739 049) and **Venini** (Piazzetta dei Leoncini, San Marco, tel: 041-522 4045; http://venini.com). In the Dorsoduro district, **Napé di F. Gambardella Gallery** (tel: 041-296 0734) sells collectors' pieces even Venetians buy, designed by virtuoso glassmakers, as well as selling quirky, everyday drinking glasses known as *'goti'*. If the official

---

⊘ CARNEVALE

The black cloak, tricorn hat, white mask and other rather sinister garb identified with Venice's Carnevale date back to the 18th century when the *commedia dell'arte* was in vogue. In the final century of the decadent, drifting Republic, Carnevale was extended to six months, and Venetians wore these costumes from December to June. Under this guise of anonymity, commoner and aristocrat were interchangeable, husbands and wives could pursue illicit love affairs. Things got so out of hand that Carnevale was eventually banned.

Today's Carnevale, revived only in 1979 and held in February/March, is more restrained. Nonetheless, this is one time of year that the city really comes to life, with street parties, masked balls, pageants, special events and visitors from all over Europe.

Murano Glass Museum is moribund, slip into **Le Stanze del Vetro** (Thu–Tue 10am–7pm; free; http://lestanzedelvetro.org) the new glass museum on the monastic island of San Giorgio, across the water from St Mark's Square. Set in the Fondazione Cini, the museum is dedicated to 20th-century and contemporary glass.

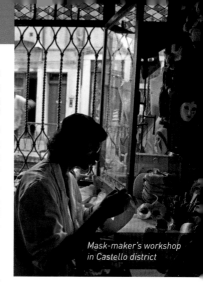

Mask-maker's workshop in Castello district

SPORTS

At the end of October, the city hosts a world-class **marathon** that attracts around 8,000 runners from across the world. If you want to participate, visit www.huaweivenicemarathon.it.

Families might prefer a summer trip to the Lido, either cycling or lapping up the private beaches. Watersports on offer include **windsurfing**, **water-skiing** and **canoeing**, or **dinghy** and **catamaran sailing**. However, swimming is not always permitted on the Lido's beaches due to pollution problems. The Lido also has an 18-hole **golf** course at Alberoni-Lido (open all year round, clubs for hire) and, in summer, **tennis** courts are open to the public.

Knowledge of the lagoon's channels is necessary for safe boating, but you can still do a **skippered cruise** or hire a boat. If, instead, you wish to try your hand at **Venetian rowing**, even for a couple of hours, contact Row Venice (www.rowvenice. com). **For kayaking in the Venetian backwaters** or exploring the wilds of the lagoon, Venice Kayak offers supervised kayak tours, even for those with very little kayaking experience (www.venicekayak.com).

CHILDREN'S VENICE

The waterways of Venice never fail to impress the young at heart, making a gondola ride a good choice for family entertainment. Best of all is a trip with **Alex Hai**, Venice's first female transgender gondolier, who does beguiling adventures (including a ghost trail http://alexhaigondolatours.com, www.gondoliera.com, primagondoliera@gmail.comalexhaigondolatours@gmail.com, tel: 388-588 8355348-302 9067). Alternatively, simply take the kids on a *vaporetto* – Venice's waterbuses offer the distinct advantage that children under four years of age travel free, and there are reduced fares for families. Excursions to the Lido, where there are beaches, water rides and pedalos, are always popular with children.

Other child-friendly options include: watching the glass-blowers at **Murano**; visiting the **Museo Storico Navale**, with its fascinating array of life-size ships or climbing up the **Campanile di San Marco**. Finally, consider a July trip to see the **Festa del Redentore** with its fabulous fireworks display (see Calendar of Events).

A fireworks show at
San Giorgio Maggiore

CALENDAR OF EVENTS

1 Jan *Capodanno* (New Year's Day) with beachfront celebrations.

Feb–Mar *Carnevale* (Carnival). Ten-day, pre-Lenten extravaganza with masked balls, processions, pantomime and music. The high point comes on Shrove Tuesday with a masked ball in Piazza San Marco, after which the effigy of Carnival is burned in the square.

25 Apr *Festa di San Marco* (St Mark's Day). Ceremonial Mass in the Basilica, when rosebuds *(bocoli)* are given as love tokens. A gondola race is also held between Sant'Elena and the Punta della Dogana, followed by a traditional soup of *risi e bisi* ('rice and peas').

Sunday after Ascension *La Sensa*, celebrating Venice's 'marriage with the sea'. Re-enacts trips made to the Lido by the doges, who cast rings into the water to symbolise the union of the Republic and the sea.

Two Sundays after Ascension *La Vogalonga* (literally: 'long row'). Hundreds of rowing boats follow a 32km (20-mile) course from the Basino di San Marco to Burano and then San Francesco del Deserto.

June–Nov *Biennale dell'Arte* (odd years only). Art exhibition held in the Arsenale and Giardini Pubblici. *Biennale Architettura* (even years only). Architecture exhibition in the same spaces.

July, third Sunday *Festa del Redentore* (Festival of the Redeemer). A sweeping bridge of boats bedecked in finery and glowing with lights stretches across the Giudecca canal to Il Redentore church. There is a spectacular firework display on the eve of the feast day.

Aug/Sept Venice hosts the International Film Festival at the Lido by day, San Marco by night.

15 Aug *Ferragosto* (Assumption). Concerts on Torcello.

Sept, first Sunday *La Regata Storica* (Historical Regatta) The finest regatta of the year, which begins with a procession up the Grand Canal led by costumed Venetians, followed by gondola races.

Nov–May Opera season at La Fenice.

21 Nov *Festa della Salute*. Processions to the candlelit Santa Maria della Salute, commemorating the city's deliverance from the plague of 1630.

EATING OUT

Venetian restaurants range in style from cool, 18th-century elegance – especially in San Marco (St Mark's) and Castello – to rustic gentility. Yet individualistic inns abound, tucked under pergolas or spilling onto terraces and courtyards. More upmarket places are termed *ristoranti*, but may be called *osterie* (inns) if they focus on simple food in an intimate or homely setting.

WHERE TO EAT

Dining in the **San Marco** area can be tricky as overpriced tourist traps, grand cafés and expensive established restaurants predominate. But moving away from St Mark's generally sees both the crowds (and the prices) fall away. Not that the grandest places should be dismissed out of hand: Venetians also patronise Harry's Bar, Florian and Quadri, at least for special occasions.

Neighbouring **Castello** offers a curious mixture of authentic inns and grandstanding luxury hotels, with sophisticated hotel restaurants to match. But hidden in alleys away from Riva degli Schiavoni are some more traditional inns.

Dorsoduro represents chic dining, but off the beaten track the district is equally well-known for its low-key cafés, tucked away in the pretty backwaters. The art galleries naturally possess sophisticated cafés, as is the case with both the Guggenheim and Punta della Dogana art collections.

Around the **Rialto market, in San Polo and Santa Croce**, look out for *bacari*, traditional Venetian tapas bars. **Cannaregio** is also studded with *bacari* as well as contemporary wine bars and everyday inns, mostly ones patronised by the Venetians.

The ones around Strada Nuova are lively by day but those around Fondamenta della Misericordia feel more alternative and tend to come alive by night.

The **outlying islands** represent some of Venice's most exciting dining areas, especially on **Giudecca and Burano**, with Giudecca far more convenient in transport terms. Here, authentic inns are interspersed with formal dining in *grande-dame* hotels,

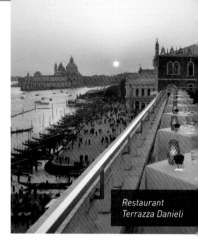

*Restaurant
Terrazza Danieli*

notably the Cipriani. Restaurants on both Giudecca and Burano are often more authentic than those clustered across the waterfront around San Marco.

VENETIAN CUISINE

Venetian food is heavily influenced by the bounty of the lagoon, with fresh fish, clams, shrimps, *calamari, seppie* (cuttlefish) and octopus all featuring heavily.

Most Venetians start the day with a coffee and croissant *(cornetto)* in a caffè, but most better-quality hotels serve a buffet breakfast, whether continental, English, or American-style.

For a light lunch, choose a *bacaro* but for a more substantial meal, opt for lunch *(pranzo)* or dinner *(cena)* in an *osteria* (inn) or *ristorante* (restaurant). A traditional feast entails up to four courses: antipasti (starters or appetisers); *primo piatto* (first

A market seller on the San Barnaba Canal

course); *secondo piatto* (main course) with *contorni* (vegetable or salad accompaniments) and *dolce* (dessert). Don't worry if you're just looking for a light bite – you certainly won't be expected to order all four courses.

Appetisers

Any trattoria worth its olive oil will offer a good selection of antipasti, either vegetarian, fish-based or meaty. A popular vegetarian choice is *carciofi* (artichokes) in season, while fish dishes include: *sarde in saor* (marinated sardines and onions, with pine kernels and raisins); *frutti di mare* (seafood), prawns, baby octopus, mussels and squid in a lemon dressing; and *vongole* (clams) or *cozze* (mussels), in a white-wine sauce. Less traditional antipasti include *carpaccio*, thin slices of raw beef dressed with olive oil; *prosciutto crudo con melone* (ham with melon); and *affettati* (charcuterie).

First course

The *primo piatto* is usually pasta, risotto or soup. In the Veneto region, pasta often takes second place to rice, and risotto is a classic Venetian dish, whether with seafood, peas, asparagus or other seasonal vegetables. Venice's most famous pasta dish is *bigoli in salsa* (pasta in an anchovy or tuna sauce) while *zuppa di pesce* (a stew-like fish soup) and *pasta e fagioli* (pasta-and-white-bean soup) are equally popular.

Main course

Seafood predominates in Venice, with *fritto misto* (mixed fried fish) or the more expensive *grigliata mista* (grilled fish) being very common. Popular fish include *coda di rospo* (monkfish), *orata* (gilt-head bream), *branzino/spigola* (seabass), *San Pietro* (John Dory) and *sogliola* (sole). More of an acquired taste is *granceola* (spidercrab served in its own shell), *anguilla alla veneziana* (eel cooked in a sauce made with lemon, oil and tuna) and *seppie al nero* (cuttlefish in its own ink) traditionally served with polenta.

    Meat dishes are rarely inspiring but one of the best bets is the Venetian favourite *fegato alla veneziana* (calf's liver with onions), served with polenta. *Vitello tonnato* (thin slices of cold veal fillet in tuna sauce) is also a good dish to try.

    Rucola (rocket) and *radicchio* (chicory/endive from Treviso) are popular components of **salads**, while assorted grilled **vegetables** are common side dishes.

    Dining can be challenging for strict vegetarians but appeal to the creativity of the chef and also try Venetian wine bars *(bacari)* such as Fiore and Alla Vedova, as well as Acqua Pazza (for pizza).

Desserts and cheese

The dessert choice is often limited to around half a dozen items, including *gelato* (ice cream) and *tiramisù* (literally 'pick me up'), a chilled creamy, coffee-flavoured concoction. *Panna cotta* ('cooked cream') has a similar texture to crème caramel, but a lighter taste. A typical Venetian custom is to serve *vino dolce con biscotti*, a glass of dessert wine with sweet biscuits.

Cheese. Strong gorgonzola is popular, often served with *parmigiano* (parmesan) or *grana*. Among the delicacies of the Veneto province is *Asiago*, a savoury, tangy cow's milk cheese.

Meal times

Most restaurants close between lunch and dinner sittings. Lunch is normally served between 12.30pm and 2.30pm, with dinner service starting around 7pm. Try to adjust to the local time in order to take the best advantage of the menu (go too late, and they may run out of things). Late-night dining can be

Spaghetti with clams and mussels

difficult to find in Venice, so you'll generally need to settle on somewhere by 9pm.

The bill usually includes service *(servizio)* of between 10 and 15 percent, but ask if you're not sure. It's normal to round the bill up slightly in addition to this.

Specials

Make it a habit to ask what specials *(piatti del giorno)* are on offer. These are often the freshest and most innovative dishes on the menu. Home-made pasta and seasonal offerings based on what's fresh from the market are typical.

WHAT TO DRINK

Depending on mood, opt for old-school glamour around San Marco or authentic, rough-and-ready Venetian wine bars *(bacari)* around the Rialto or Cannaregio, bursting with tasty treats to detain you from dinner.

In Venice, local Veneto wines predominate, from sparkling Prosecco, the perfect *aperitif*, to crisp Soave, Valpolicella or Bardolino. The Bellini, a combination of Prosecco and fresh peach juice, was supposedly invented in Harry's Bar, still a stylish spot for cocktails near San Marco. The other classic local cocktail is spritz, an orangey concoction made of Campari or bitters, white wine and soda water. To widen your wine knowledge, look out for an *enoteca*, a combination of wine bar and wine merchant, a cosy spot that probably also serves snacks.

Bars of San Marco

For old-school glamour, the waterfront-hotel piano bars have been playing the same tune for centuries. But if you can resist the tinkling from these *grande-dame* bars, drink in a sunset view from the **Terrazza Danieli** *(Danieli Hotel)* before the bar criminally closes at 6.30pm. Then try the legendary **Harry's Bar** (Calle Vallaresso).

For an atmospheric waterside bar, call into the next *calle* to sip a Prosecco on the pontoon at **Ca' Giustinian** (Calle del Ridotto), a Gothic palace with sweeping views over to La Salute. Now the headquarters of the Biennale, it was once the hotel where Turner, Proust and Verdi all found artistic inspiration. The chic set also feels utterly at home in the **B-Bar** (L'Hotel Bauer, Campo San Moise), where the gold mosaics reflect the glitterati in all their glory. Finally, call it a night at **Caffè Centrale** if only to conclude that glamorous, night-owl Venice exists, contrary to rumour. Definitely down a Manhattan, not a Venetian spritz.

⊙ A VENETIAN WINE CRAWL

Bacari are traditional wine bars that also serve a Venetian version of tapas, known as *cicchetti*. A *bacari* crawl, especially in the authentic Rialto or Cannaregio areas, represents one of the highlights of any stay in Venice. When planning a route, be influenced by neighbourhood, mood and personal taste for authenticity, tranquillity or live music. Known as a *giro di ombre*, a bar crawl is best begun at sunset as some of the more traditional bars close early. These time-warp taverns are the perfect introduction to *cicchetti*, from slivers of dried salt cod *(baccala)* slathered on *crostini*, to tiny meatballs or sweet and sour sardines – usually washed down with Prosecco. Other cheap but often sensational tapas include *calamari*, marinated radicchio, fried mozzarella balls, asparagus tarts, Venetian sushi, or shrimp wrapped in pancetta.

TO HELP YOU ORDER

Waiter/waitress **Cameriere/cameriera**
Do you have a set menu? **Avete un menù a prezzo fisso?**
I'd like a/an/some ... **Vorrei ...**

beer **una birra**
bread **del pane**
butter **del burro**
coffee **un caffè**
cream **della panna**
fish **del pesce**
fruit **della frutta**
ice cream **un gelato**
meat **della carne**
milk **del latte**

pepper **del pepe**
potatoes **delle patate**
salad **un'insalata**
salt **del sale**
soup **una minestra**
sugar **dello zucchero**
tea **un tè**
water (mineral) **dell'acqua (minerale)**
wine **del vino**

MENU READER

aglio garlic
agnello lamb
albicocche apricots
aragosta lobster
arancia orange
bistecca beefsteak
carciofi artichokes
cipolle onions
crostacei shellfish
fiche figs
formaggio cheese
frutti di mare seafood
funghi mushrooms
lamponi raspberries
maiale pork
manzo beef

mela apple
melanzane aubergine
merluzzo cod
ostriche oysters
pesca peach
pollo chicken
pomodori tomatoes
prosciutto ham
seppie cuttlefish
tacchino turkey
tonno tuna
uovo egg
uva grapes
verdure vegetables
vitello veal
vongole clams

PLACES TO EAT

We have used the following symbols to give an idea of the price for a two-course meal for one, including house wine and service:

€€€€	over €85
€€€	€55–85
€€	€25–55
€	up to €25

SAN MARCO

Acqua Pazza €€–€€€ *Campo Sant'Angelo, San Marco 3808, tel: 041-277 0688; www.veniceacquapazza.com, Apr–Oct daily, Nov–Mar closed Mon.* This slick, upmarket spot on a trendy square is the place for huge pizzas or fine seafood when Venetian squid ink is too exotic to contemplate. A post-coffee Limoncello is on the house. Vaporetto: S. Angelo.

Caffè Centrale €€€ *Piscina Frezzeria, San Marco 1659b, tel: 041-887 6642; www.caffecentralevenezia.com, daily 7pm–1am.* This sleek lounge bar, late-night restaurant and music club feels more Milanese or Manhattanite than Venetian, albeit with gondola attached. Set in a converted cinema, the moody *palazzo* mixes modish cuisine and cutting-edge design. Vaporetto: San Marco Vallaresso.

Cavatappi €€ *Campo della Guerra, near San Zulian, San Marco 525, tel: 041-296 0252, daily.* A fashionable, contemporary-style wine bar serving *cicchetti*, light lunches and evening meals; trust the specials and the wines. Vaporetto: San Zaccaria or Rialto.

Grancaffè Quadri €€ *Piazza San Marco, tel: 041-522 2105; www.alajmo.it/grancaffe-quadri, daily.* Founded in 1683, this baroque grand café is a Venetian institution, perfect for people-watching over a wintry hot chocolate and cakes or cocktails and nibbles (Quadri's gourmet restaurant upstairs €€€€). Vaporetto: San Marco Vallaresso.

Harry's Bar €€€€ *Calle Vallaresso 1323, San Marco 1323, tel: 041-528 5777*; http://cipriani.com, *daily.* The consistency of this legendary bar and restaurant also draws a resolutely Venetian crowd. The unpretentious tone (if not the price) is perfect. Sip a Bellini (Prosecco and peach juice, invented here), even if the price puts you off having a second. Vaporetto: San Marco Vallaresso.

Ristorante Do Forni €€€ *Calle degli Specchieri, tel: 041-523 2148*; www.doforni.it, *daily.* An upmarket but old-school spot with rambling yet intimate rooms. There is plenty of atmosphere but no views. The menu embraces Italian classics along with international and Venetian dishes. Vaporetto: San Marco Giardinetti.

CASTELLO

Alle Testiere €€€ *Calle del Mondo Novo, Castello 5801, tel: 041-522 7220*; www.osterialletestiere.it, *closed Sun and Mon.* Located near Campo Santa Maria Formosa, this renowned seafood restaurant demands booking (few tables). The menu harks back to Venice's days on the Oriental spice route; razor clams or pasta may be subtly spiced; fine wine list. Vaporetto: San Zaccaria.

Al Covo €€€–€€€€ *Campiello della Pescaria, tel: 041-522 3812*; http://ristorantealcovo.com, *closed Wed and Thu.* Covo's fine reputation draws foodies to sample the fish-heavy tasting menu. The *moeche* (softshell crab) lightly fried with onions vie with Adriatic tuna, or squid-ink pasta with clams and courgette flowers. Booking essential for this formal spot. Vaporetto: Arsenale.

Enoteca Mascareta €€ *Calle Lunga Santa Maria Formosa, tel: 041-523 0744*; www.ostemaurolorenzon.com, *daily 7pm–2am.* A cosy, rustic wine bar run by an eccentric wine buff host. Nibble on charcuterie at the counter, or opt for the small, changing menu. Expect a laid-back jazz atmosphere and superb wines. If you're still hungry, head to **Al Mascaron** next-door. Vaporetto: Rialto.

L'Osteria di Santa Marina €€€ *Campo Santa Marina, tel: 041-528 5239;* http://osteriadisantamarina.com, *closed all Sun and Mon lunch.* Set in a quiet square, this deceptively simple trattoria presents reinterpretations of Venetian classics, from cuttlefish ink ravioli with sea bass to seafood pasta, fresh turbot, tuna, and beef carpaccio, tuna-and-bean soup and mixed grills. Finish with a sorbet or cinnamon apple pie. Vaporetto: Rialto.

DORSODURO

Cantinone già Schiavi € *Fondamenta Nani, Rio di San Trovaso, tel: 041-523 0034;* www.cantinaschiavi.com, *Mon–Sat 8.30am–8.30pm.* This old-fashioned canalside wine bar is overly popular with Venetians and visitors from all walks of life. It's a good place for grazing on *cicchetti* – among the most inventive in Venice. Savour the mood by propping up the bar over a light lunch or lingering over canalside cocktails (7–8pm). Vaporetto: Zattere.

Oniga €€ *Campo San Barnaba, tel: 041-522 4410;* www.oniga.it, *daily.* Dine inside or on the campo after opting for the Venetian seafood platter or the vegetarian option. For once, vegetarians can be spoilt with an array of pasta dishes made with artichokes, aubergines and pecorino cheese. Vaporetto: Ca' Rezzonico.

Osteria Ca' del Vento €€ *Calle del Vento, tel: 041-850 1909;* www.osteriacadelvento.it, *closed Tue.* This atmospheric family-run restaurant is slightly off the beaten track and serves up traditional Italian fare, all based on fresh local produce. A lot of vegetarian options available. It's a small restaurant and popular with the locals, so it's best to book in advance. Vaporetto: San Basilio.

SAN POLO AND SANTA CROCE

Alla Madonna €€–€€€ *Calle della Madonna, tel: 041-522 3824;* www.ristoranteallamadonna.com, *closed Wed.* This arty, bustling, ever-popular trattoria (no reservations) serves meticulously prepared seafood, fresh from the lagoon. Tuck into Sant'Erasmo artichokes or a seafood risotto while also being seduced by the impressive art collection. Vaporetto: Rialto Mercato.

Alla Zucca €€ *Ponte del Megio, off Campo San Giacomo dell'Orio, tel: 041-524 1570; www.lazucca.it, closed Sun.* This popular trattoria is set by a crooked canal bridge, with a few tables outside. The bohemian atmosphere reflects the vegetable-inspired menu (aubergine pasta, smoked ricotta, pumpkin flan) as well as meat and fish. Booking advisable. Vaporetto: San Stae.

Cantina Do Spade € *Calle delle Do Spade, Rialto, tel: 041-521 0583; http://cantinadospade.com, closed Tue morning.* One of the oldest Rialto *bacari* is still going strong. Expect deep-fried *calamari*, *baccala* (salted cod), meatballs and other typical *cicchetti* (tapas). Stand at the bar and chat to Venetians or grab a table for a traditional meal. The service is prompt and friendly. Vaporetto: Rialto Mercato.

Da Fiore €€€€ *Calle del Scaleter, off Campo di San Polo, tel: 041-721 308; www.dafiore.net, closed Sun and Mon.* Regularly dubbed the best restaurant in town, this reflects the subtlety of Venetian cuisine, from grilled calamari and *granseola* (spider crab) to Adriatic tuna, squid, sashimi and *risotto al nero di seppia* (cuttlefish risotto). Vaporetto: San Tomà.

Ristorante Ribot €€ *Fondamenta Minotto, Rio del Gaffaro, Santa Croce, tel: 041-534 3126, daily.* This authentic neighbourhood restaurant is superb value (try the risotto, grilled scallops or seafood pasta) but also has a secret garden, and live music in the evening. Piazzale Roma (Station).

CANNAREGIO

Algiubagio €€ *Fondamenta Nuove 5039, tel: 041-523 6084; www.algiubagio.net.* This contemporary *bacaro* is the perfect place for flirting over *cicchetti*, or for waiting for the ferry to Murano, Burano or the airport (via Alilaguna). A good but pricier restaurant attached. Vaporetto: Fondamenta Nuove.

Alla Frasca € *Cannaregio 5176, tel: 041-241 2585, closed Wed.* Hidden in the backstreets, this friendly, genuine inn serves fresh, no-frills local cuisine; dine on grilled fish or spaghetti with clams in the pretty courtyard and finally feel like a Venetian. Vaporetto: Fondamenta Nuove.

Al Vecio Bragosso €€ *Strada Nuova, Cannaregio 4386, tel: 041-523 7277;* www.alveciobragosso.com, *daily.* The family has a fishing *bragozzo* (hence the name), which hauls in fresh seafood each day. Try the Venetian *sardèle in soar* (sardines in an onion sauce with pinenuts and raisins). Vaporetto: Ca' d'Oro.

Ca Dolfin €€ *Cannaregio 5903, tel: 041-528 5299, daily.* Set near the Rialto Bridge, this is a favourite among local gourmets and tourists alike for authentic Italian food. The sea bass with courgettes and peppers and spaghetti with mussels are really worth a try, just as the rest of the menu. It's pet-friendly too. The restaurant is rather small, so booking is recommended. Vaporetto: Rialto.

Da Rioba €€ *Fondamenta della Misericordia, tel: 041-524 4379, closed Mon.* This rustic-chic restaurant is set on a canal that comes alive at night, and you can dine outside, by the bustling waterfront. The cooking is subtly creative – whether with pasta dishes or with seafood, including tuna carpaccio. Vaporetto: San Marcuola.

Vini da Gigio €€ *Fondamenta di San Felice, tel: 041-528 5140;* www.vinidagigio.com, *closed Mon and Tue.* Both cosy and romantic, this popular family-run inn serves reliable Slow Food with leisurely service. There's lots of variety, from Venetian risotto to northern Italian game dishes, as well as fine wines. Booking advisable. Vaporetto: Ca' d'Oro.

GIUDECCA

Altanella €€€ *Calle delle Erbe, tel: 041-522 7780, closed Mon and Tue.* Friendly trattoria favoured by Elton John, who has a home around the corner. Only fish dishes on offer, but also try the ice cream with grappa-soaked raisins. Lovely outdoor seating with sweeping views across the Giudecca Canal. No credit cards. Vaporetto: Palanca or Redentore.

Harry's Dolci €€€ *Fondamenta San Biagio, tel: 041-522 4844;* http://cipriani.com, *daily.* Come here for a waterside American brunch; it's Harry's without the hype, and with better views and prices. Try the Venetian risotto or, better still, come for cakes *(dolci)* outside mealtimes, or sip a signature Bellini in the bar. Vaporetto: Sant' Eufemia.

Skyline Rooftop Bar €€€ *Molino Stucky Hilton, Fondamenta San Biagio 810, tel: 041-272 3316;* www.skylinebarvenice.it, *daily summer until 1am, winter until midnight.* Come for the scenery, not the food, but it all tastes fine in such a setting, with rooftop pool and views over the long tail-shaped island of Giudecca. Venetians make one (pricey) Bellini last and then head to somewhere more substantial. Vaporetto: Palanca.

THE OTHER ISLANDS

Alla Maddalena €€ *Fondamenta di Santa Caterina 7C, Mazzorbo, tel: 041-730 151;* www.trattoriamaddalena.com, *closed Thu.* Dine here for a superbly creative menu inspired by Veneto cuisine, Slow Food values and very local wines. That's if you're not tempted by **Venissa** next door (see page 139). Vaporetto: ferry 41/42 from Fondamenta Nuove to Mazzorbo, then cross the footbridge.

Al Ponte del Diavolo €€–€€€ *Fondamenta Borgognoni 10, Isola di Torcello, tel: 041-730 401;* www.osteriaalpontedeldiavolo.com, *lunch only, closed Mon.* Set on Torcello, this inn is a charming rustic lunch venue. Vaporetto from Fondamenta Nuove to Torcello.

Al Raspo De Ua €€ *Via Galuppi 560, Isola di Burano, tel; 041-730 095;* www.alraspodeua.it, *lunch only, daily.* This is a people-watching spot on the main piazza in Burano and the place for pasta with prawns, then Vin Santo dessert wine with Burano's *buranelli* biscuits. Vaporetto: ferry service from Fondamenta Nuove to Burano.

Trattoria alle Vignole €–€€ *Isola Vignole 12, tel: 041-528 9707, private boat.* For an adventure, take a water taxi or private boat (it's not on any vaporetto route) to the island of Le Vignole. Moor alongside the garden gates and eat razor clams and courgette flowers.

A–Z TRAVEL TIPS

A SUMMARY OF PRACTICAL INFORMATION

A

ACCOMMODATION

Even if Venice has its fair share of palatial hotels, there is now great choice at the more modest end, from boutique retreats to chic guesthouses, eclectic B&Bs, Gothic apartments under the eaves, or intimate, family-owned *palazzi*. The lack of standardisation in Venetian hotels cuts both ways: each room is delightfully different but, on the other hand, even in a distinguished hotel, the rooms at the front may be glorious, but hide dingy garrets at the back. (See page 131.)

Apartments: These make a delightful way of experiencing the real city, even revelling in a Gothic *palazzo* complete with gondola dock. **Venetian Apartments** (www.veniceprestige.com, tel: (+44) 020-3356 9667) are the market leaders, with a reliable range of fully-vetted apartments to suit couples, families or even celebratory house parties.

B&Bs: This is an effective way of getting to meet real Venetians. For a wide range of bed and breakfasts, see BB Planet (www.bbplanet.it) and check by district and price.

Outside central Venice: Apart from Giudecca, consider the islands of Burano, Murano and the Lido. If staying outside the city, avoid soulless Mestre and opt for atmospheric Padua or Treviso, a 30-minute train ride from Venice.

Advance booking is essential during peak periods when some hotels are booked up months in advance: at Carnival, April to June, September and October and Christmas and New Year.

I'd like a single/double room **Vorrei una camera singola/ matrimoniale**
with (without) bath/shower **con (senza) bagno/doccia**
What's the rate per night? **Qual è il prezzo per una notte?**

AIRPORTS

Venice Marco Polo airport (VCE); tel: 041-260 9260; www.veniceairport. it) lies 13km (8 miles) north of the city.

Public buses (ACTV; http://actv.avmspa.it) run from the airport to the terminus at Piazzale Roma every quarter of an hour throughout most of the day; airport buses (ATVO; www.atvo.it) run every half-hour, have a similar journey time (about 20–25 minutes) and price (€8 single, €15 return). Buy tickets online or from the ATVO office in the arrivals terminal. Once at Piazzale Roma, board the No. 1 *vaporetto* (waterbus) for an all-stages ride along the Grand Canal; or take the No. 2 for the quickest route to San Marco. The Ponte Calatrava also connects you by foot to the main railway station.

Public water launches: Alilaguna (www.alilaguna.it) is the shuttle connecting Venice and the airport (€27 return); key routes are Blue (Blu), Orange (Arancio), Red (Rosso; seasonal route): the Blue line goes to Fondamenta Nuove (40 minutes) while the Orange Line runs to San Marco (90 minutes).

Private water taxis: the speediest and most stylish way to arrive (30 minutes, from €100) and they take you right up to your hotel if it has a water entrance.

Treviso (TSF; www.trevisoairport.it) is a small airport 32km (20 miles) north of Venice, used by charters and low-cost airlines such as Ryanair, who, confusingly, call it 'Venice airport'. ATVO's Treviso Airport Bus Express runs between Treviso airport and Venice's Piazzale Roma (€22 return).

Where's the boat/bus for...? **Dove si prende il vaporetto/ l'autobus per...?**
I want a ticket to... **Desidero uno biglietto per...**
What time does the train/bus leave for the city centre? **A che ora parte il treno/pullman per il centro?**

B

BUDGETING FOR YOUR TRIP

Airport transfer from Marco Polo. By road: public bus (ACTV) €8; taxi €40 (for up to four people). By water: Alilaguna public water launch €27 return per person; private water taxi approximately €150 for four people and luggage.

The Chorus Pass (www.chorusvenezia.org or www.veneziaunica.it) allows access to 16 Venetian churches (including the Frari), with charges going towards local church restoration. The price of a normal pass is €12 per person.

Entertainment. A concert in a main church costs from €25; Fenice opera tickets from €100. Casino admission €5–10.

Gondolas. From €80–150 (depending on duration, time of day and services).

Guided tours. For a walking tour, allow around €25.

Food. *Tramezzini* (small sandwiches) from €4; *cichetti* (hot and cold tapas at wine bars) from €4 per item; full meal for one at an inexpensive restaurant €25–30; at a moderate restaurant, including cover and service (excluding drinks) €40–5; pizza €8–15; beer €3–5; glass of house wine €2–5.

Hotel. For bed and breakfast per night in high season, inclusive of tax: deluxe €400 and above; expensive, €280–400; moderate, €150–280; inexpensive, less than €150.

Lido beaches: from €10 (from the morning, including sunbed/parasol) but only around €3 after 2pm.

Museums and attractions. €4–20 (see page 127).

Public transport: €60 for 7 days, €40 for 3 days, €30 for 2 days, €20 for 1 day (24 hours). A ticket valid for 75 minutes costs €7.50.

C

CLIMATE

Venetian winters are cold, summers are hot, and the weather the rest of the year somewhere in between. The winds off the Adriatic and occasional flooding mean that Venice can be damp and chilly, although very atmospheric, between November and March. June, July and August can be stifling – air conditioning is pretty essential for a good night's rest at this time of year.

	J	F	M	A	M	J	J	A	S	O	N	D
Max												
°F	42	46	54	63	71	77	83	83	79	65	54	46
°C	6	8	12	17	22	25	28	28	26	18	12	8
Min												
°F	34	34	41	51	57	64	68	66	62	52	43	37
°C	1	1	5	10	14	18	20	19	17	11	6	3

CLOTHING

A pair of comfortable walking shoes is essential – you'll probably spend most of your time on foot. For summer, pack thin cotton clothing and a light jacket for breezy evening *vaporetto* rides. While visiting churches, your back and shoulders need to be covered. For winter trips, pack layers, including a warm coat. Smart hotels lend waterproof boots in case of light flooding. Venice is generally an informal city, but stylish dress is expected at smarter restaurants and piano bars, including those at the more elegant hotels. Men must wear a jacket and tie to gain entry to the Casino.

CRIME AND SAFETY (see also Emergencies and Police)

Although Venice is incredibly safe, pickpockets are not uncommon, especially in the crowded areas around the Rialto and San Marco. Carry only what is absolutely necessary; leave the rest in the hotel safe. Make photocopies of your passport and other vital documents to facilitate reporting any theft and obtaining replacements. Notify the police of any theft, so that they can give you a statement to file with your insurance claim.

I want to report a theft **Voglio denunciare un furto**

D

DRIVING

Venice is a **traffic-free zone**, and the closest you can get to the centre in a car is Piazzale Roma, where there are two large multi-storey car parks and good ferry services (http://avm.avmspa.it). There is also a huge multi-storey car park on the adjacent island of Tronchetto, the terminal for the car ferry to the Lido, where driving is allowed. Tronchetto (tel: 041-520 7555, www.veniceparking.it) is linked to Venice (Piazzale Roma) via the new monorail, called the People Mover. Although the outdoor car parks are guarded night and day, it's sensible not to leave anything of value in your car.

E

ELECTRICITY

The electrical current is 220V, AC, and sockets take two-pin round-pronged plugs. Bring an adaptor *(un adattatore)*, as required.

EMBASSIES AND CONSULATES

Most consulates have useful lists of English-speaking doctors, lawyers and interpreters, etc.

Australia: Via Borgogna 2, Milan, tel: 027-767 4200, https://italy.embassy.gov.au.

Canada: Piazza Cavour 3, Milan; tel: 026-269 4238, www.canadainternational.gc.ca.

New Zealand: Via Clitunno 44, Rome; tel: 06-853 7501, www.mfat.govt.nz/en/embassies.

Republic of Ireland: Villa Spada, Via Giacomo Medici 1, Rome; tel: 06-

585 2381, www.dfa.ie/irish-embassy/italy.

South Africa (honorary consulate): Via Locchi 10, Trieste, tel: 040 30 07 61, http://lnx.sudafrica.it.

UK: Via XX Settembre 80/a, Rome, tel: 06-4220 0001, www.gov.uk/world/organisations/british-embassy-rome.

US: via Principe Amedeo 2/10, Milan; tel: 02-290 351, https://it.usembassy.gov.

EMERGENCIES

In case of an emergency, tel: Ambulance: **118**; Fire: **115**; Carabinieri: **112** (urgent police action); Police: **113**

G

GETTING THERE

By air. Companies flying from the UK include British Airways (www.britishairways.com), easyJet (www.easyjet.com), Ryanair (www.ryanair.com) and TUI Airways (www.tui.co.uk). Ryanair also run flights to Treviso airport (32km/20 miles from Venice) from several UK destinations, including London Southend. Aer Lingus (www.aerlingus.com) operate services from Dublin to Venice. From the US there are direct flights from New York (Delta Airlines, www.delta.com) and other gateways through Alitalia (www.alitalia.it).

By train. Venice's Stazione Venezia – Santa Lucia is well-connected to Turin, Milan, Florence and Rome, as well as to Paris, Vienna and London. Arriving by train can be a romantic experience, with the slowness offset by wonderful views through France and within sight of the Alps. Travel via Eurostar/Thello – departing London 1.31pm and arriving in Venice at 9.35am the following day, or book a rail pass (International Rail, tel. +44 0871 231 0790, www.internationalrail.com).

GUIDES AND TOURS

Try an art tour or see the progress on the famous MOSE Mobile Barrier at the entrance to the Lido. Watch snoozing sunbathers on their boats and greet local fishermen from Burano before exploring islands which couldn't be more different from one another.

Culture: Accademia Gallery: for booking tickets at set times or for booking individual art tours (tel: 041-520 0345, www.gallerieac-cademia.it). **St Mark's and the Doge's Palace:** Free tours are given of the Basilica in summer, while **'Secret Routes'** (Itinerari Segreti; booking essential, tel: 041-4273 0892, http://palazzoducale.visitmuve.it) show you the ins and outs of life at the Palazzo Ducale.

Ghost tours: for an unusual walking tour of Venice's backstreets and alleys try Veltra CityDiscovery (www.veltra.com). Venice ghost tours: 7pm Mon, Wed, Fri or Sat, meeting at Campo San Bartolomeo.

Brenta Canal cruise: a cruise to Padua aboard the 200-seater Burchiel-lo (www.burchiello.it) motorboat traces how the Venetian nobility once lived in their summer villas.

Lagoon tours: Destination Venice (Campo San Luca, San Marco 4590, tel: 041-528 3547, www.destination-venice.com) offer made-to-meas-ure explorations of the lagoon and islands, along with individual guided walks, and Venetian-style rowing lessons. Thanks to the shifting tides and the shallowness of the lagoon, the islands preserve a pastoral way of life, one that is rarely visible to visitors who stay close to the shore. The lagoon is often dismissed as a desolate marsh but it is also a patch-work of sand banks, salt pans and mud flats, with sections cultivated as fish farms, market gardens and vineyards much lagoon life survives, from kingfishers, cormorants and coots to grey herons and egrets. This is where Venetians retreat to go fishing, watch birds and sunbathe. At low tide, the shrimp fishermen leave their boats and seem to walk across water; families picnicking on remote sandbanks appear from nowhere and then disappear again with the tide.

Venice Kayak (tel: +39 346 477 1327, www.venicekayak.com) offers re-freshingly untouristy kayak tours around the city and lagoon, including seeing the sights from the water. Do day or night paddles from their base at Certosa Island, easily reached by *vaporetto* (€125 per person per day).

H

HEALTH AND MEDICAL CARE

EU residents: obtain an EHIC (European Health Insurance Card), available online at www.ehic.org.uk, which provides emergency medical/hospital (*ospedale*) treatment by reciprocal agreement. These arrangements are all subject to change after Brexit; check these details before departing.

For US citizens: if your private health insurance policy does not cover you while abroad, take out a short-term policy before leaving home.

Medical emergencies: Ask at your hotel or consulate if you need a doctor/dentist who speaks English. The **Guardia Medica** (tel: 041-529 4060) is a night call-out service. Many doctors at Ospedale SS. Giovanni e Paolo, Venice's only hospital, next to San Zanipolo, speak English; tel: 041-529 4111 (and ask for *'pronto soccorso'*, A&E/casualty).

Mosquitoes: a nuisance in Venice in summer, solved with a small plug-in machine.

Pharmacies: Italian *farmacie* open during shopping hours and in turn for night and holiday service; the address of the nearest open pharmacy is posted on all pharmacy doors.

I need a doctor/dentist **Ho bisogno di un medico/dentista**
I've a pain here **Ho un dolore qui**
a stomach ache **il mal di stomaco**
a fever **la febbre**

L

LANGUAGE

Most Venetian hotels and shops will have staff who speak some English, French or German. However, in bars and cafés away from Piazza San Marco, you'll almost certainly have the chance to practise your Italian.

M

MAPS

Despite its watery character, Venice is made for walking. Weave your way around on foot, with brief forays on ferries that circle the city or whisk you to the outer reaches of the lagoon. Addresses can be bewildering, labelled by just the street number and neighbourhood: if in doubt, ask the name of the closest parish church; this is more helpful than the postal address. But still expect to get lost in this labyrinthine city.

MEDIA

For Venice listings, must-see places and activities, check www.timeout.com/venice and www.inyourpocket.com/venice.

MONEY

Italy's monetary unit is the euro (€), which is divided into 100 cents. Banknotes are available in denominations of 500, 200, 100, 50, 20, 10 and 5 euro. There are coins for 2 and 1 euro, and for 50, 20, 10, 5, 2 and 1 cents.

Currency exchange. *Bureau de change* offices *(cambi)* are usually open Monday to Friday, although hours do vary (Travelex offices at Piazza San Marco and the airport). Both *cambi* and banks charge a commission. Banks generally offer higher exchange rates and lower commissions. Passports are usually required when changing money.

ATMs and credit cards. Automatic currency-exchange machines *(bancomat)* are operated by most banks and can also be found in the centre of town. Most hotels, shops and restaurants take credit cards.

O

OPENING TIMES

Banks. Hours are Mon–Fri 8.30am–1.30pm, 2.45–4pm.
Bars and restaurants. Some café-bars open for breakfast, but others do

not open until around noon; the vast majority shut early, at around 10.30 or 11pm. Old-fashioned *bacari* (wine and tapas bars) in the Rialto area often close early (at around 9.30pm). Most restaurants close at least one day a week; some close for parts of August, January and February.

Churches. The majority of the 16 Chorus Churches are open Mon–Sat 10.30am–4.30pm. The Frari is also open Sun 1–6pm. Other churches are normally open Mon–Sat from around 8am until noon and from 3 or 4pm until 6 or 7pm. On Sunday, some are only open for morning services.

Museums and galleries. Most close on Monday, but are otherwise open at 9 or 10am until 6pm.

Shops. Business hours are Monday to Saturday, 9 or 10am until 1pm, and 3 or 4pm until 7pm. Some shops are open all day and even on Sundays, particularly in peak season.

P

POLICE

Although you rarely see them, Venice's police (*Polizia* or *Carabinieri*) function efficiently and are courteous. The emergency police telephone number is **112** or **113**; this will put you through to a switchboard and someone who speaks your language.

> Where's the nearest police station? **Dov'è il più vicino posto di polizia?**

POST OFFICES

The most convenient post office is on the Rialto (Calle San Salvador 5106, San Marco, Mon–Fri 8.20am–7.05pm, Sat 8.20am–12.35pm), and on Lista di Spagna 233 (Cannaregio, Mon–Sat 8.20am–1.35pm). Postage stamps *(francobolli)* are sold at post offices and tobacconists *(tabacchi)*, marked by a distinctive 'T' sign.

PUBLIC HOLIDAYS

Banks, government offices and most shops and museums close on public holidays (*giorni festivi*). When a major holiday falls on a Thursday or a Tuesday, Italians may make a *ponte* (bridge) to the weekend, meaning that Friday or Monday is taken, too.

The most important holidays are:

1 January **Capodanno** New Year
6 January **Epifania** (Epiphany)
25 April **Festa della Liberazione** Liberation Day
1 May **Festa del Lavoro** (Labour Day)
15 August **Ferragosto** (Assumption)
1 November **Ognissanti** (All Saints)
8 December **Immacolata Concezione** (Immaculate Conception)
25 December **Natale** (Christmas Day)
26 December **Santo Stefano** (Boxing Day)
Moveable Date **Pasquetta** (Easter Monday)

The **Festa della Salute** on 21 November and the **Redentore** on the third Sunday of July are special Venetian holidays, when many shops close.

R

RELIGION

Although predominantly Roman Catholic, Venice has congregations of all the major religions.

Anglican. Church of St George, Campo San Vio, Dorsoduro.
Evangelical Lutheran. Campo Santi Apostoli, Cannaregio.
Evangelical Waldensian/Methodist. Santa Maria Formosa, Castello.
Greek Orthodox. Ponte dei Greci, Castello.
Jewish Synagogue. Campo del Ghetto Vecchio, Cannaregio.
Roman Catholic. Basilica San Marco; Masses in Italian; confession in several languages.

T

TELEPHONES

The country code for Italy is 39, and the area code for the city of Venice is 041. Note that you must dial the '041' prefix even when making local calls within the city of Venice. Note that smaller bars and businesses increasingly only have mobile numbers.

Mobile phones. EU mobile (cell) phones can be used in Italy, but check compatibility or buy an Italian SIM card, available from any mobile phone shop, if you intend to stay for long. Mobile phone use in EU countries is now included in most plans for no extra cost but to be sure check with your local GSM dealer for information on roaming costs before visiting.

International Calls. Dial 00, followed by the country code (Australia +61, Ireland +353, New Zealand +64, South Africa +27, UK +44, US and Canada +1), then the area code (often minus the initial zero) and finally the individual number.

TIME

Italy is one hour ahead of Greenwich Mean Time (GMT). From the last Sunday in March to the last Sunday in October, clocks are put forward an hour.

TIPPING

A service charge of 10 or 12 percent is often added to restaurant bills, so it is not necessary to tip much – perhaps just round the bill up. However, it is normal to tip bellboys, porters, tour guides and elderly gondoliers who help you into and out of your craft posted at the landing stations.

TOILETS

There are public toilets *(toilette, gabinetti)* usually with a charge, at the airport and railway station. Most people use the facilities in bars but only if you order a drink. *Signori* means men; *signore* means women.

> Where are the toilets? **Dove sono i gabinetti?**

TOURIST INFORMATION

The Italian National Tourist Board has several offices abroad which may provide basic information:

Australia: Level 2, 140 William Street, Sydney; tel: 02-9357 2561; www.enit.it.

Canada: 365 Bay Street, Suite 503, Toronto (Ontario) M5H 2V1; tel: 416-925 4882; www.enit.it.

UK/Ireland: 1 Princes Street, London W1B 2AY; tel: 020-7408 1254; www.enit.it.

US: www.italiantourism.com.

Los Angeles: 10850 Wilshire Blvd., Suite 575, Los Angeles, CA 90024; tel: 310-820 1898; www.enit.it.

New York: 686 Park Avenue, New York, NY 10065, tel: 212 245 5618; www.enit.it.

Tourist information offices in Venice. The best tourist office (APT) is in the **Venice Pavilion** (tel: 041-529 8730) beside the Giardinetti Reali (Public Gardens), with a good Venice bookshop. The hard-working but under-staffed office is open daily 10am–6pm. There is another one on the western corner of **Piazza San Marco**, opposite the Museo Correr: San Marco 71/f, Calle dell'Ascensione/Procuratie Nuove; daily 9am–3.30pm. Both offices tend to charge for maps, events listings and other brochures. They also offer booking for tours and events. There are tourist offices at the railway station (**APT Venezia, Stazione Santa Lucia**), and at the airport: **APT Marco Polo**, which mostly deals with accommodation and transport tickets.

TRANSPORT

Vaporetti (water buses). These workhorses will take you to within a short walk of anywhere you want to visit. The main waterbus services are: **No. 1**, which stops at every landing stage along the Grand Canal; **No. 2,** provides a faster service down the Grand Canal as part of its circular San Marco,

Giudecca canal, Piazzale Roma route (and the Lido). **Nos 4.1** (anticlockwise) and **4.2** (clockwise) describe Venice in a circular route, calling at San Zaccaria, Il Redentore (Palladio's masterpiece), Piazzale Roma, Ferrovia (the railway station), Fondamenta Nuove, San Michele, Murano and Sant'Elena. Vaporetti **5.1 and 5.2** also provide long, scenic, circular tours around the periphery, as well as stopping at Murano; in summer they go on to the Lido (change at Fondamenta Nuove to do the whole route). Note that the circular routes travel up the Cannaregio canal, stopping at Guglie, and then skirting the northern shores of Venice, including Fondamenta Nuove and the Madonna dell'Orto (Tintoretto's church), the shipyards (Bacini stop), San Pietro di Castello and, eventually, the Lido. **No. 6** provides a fast route between Piazzale Roma and the Lido, going via the Zattere (Giudecca canal). Hop on the lagoon lines **(Nos 11, 12, 13, 14, 15, 20 and 22)** to get to the outer islands, including Murano and Burano. **Line 9** connects Burano with Torcello.

Gondolas. The official daytime rate is €80 for 40 mins (up to six people), then €40–50 for each subsequent 20 mins. The evening rate (from 8pm–8am) is €100. Inauthentic serenaded gondola tours (40 mins) are €44 per person.

Water taxis (*motoscafi*). These are for a door-to-door service that comes with a high cost.

Traghetti. The *traghetto* (gondola ferry, locals 70 cents, tourists €2) operates at key points across the Grand Canal. It is customary (but not obligatory) to stand while crossing.

Walking. It is often quicker (and cheaper) to walk so enjoy getting lost on foot: official addresses are confusing so always ask for the name of the nearest church or square (*campo*).

When's the next *vaporetto* for...? **A che ore parte il prossimo vaporetto per...?**
What's the fare to...? **Quanto costa il biglietto per...?**
I want a ticket to... **Vorrei un biglietto per...**

A water **transport map** (€3) is available from all Venice tourist offices, and from Venezia Unica offices (including on Piazza San Marco, tel. 041-2424, www.veneziaunica.it). Check ferry routes on the public ACTV water transport site (http://actv.avmspa.it), which is reliable for maps, timetables and ferry routes for the *vaporetti* (waterbuses).

ACTV Pass (including islands) pre-bookable: €60 for 7 days, €40 for 3 days, €30 for 2 days, €20 for 24 hours; €7.50 for a 75-minute journey (passes discounted on www.veneziaunica.it). Before every journey, swipe your pass by holding the rechargeable electronic card up to the sensor by the boarding pier: a green light and a bleep means the pass is valid; otherwise seek assistance.

Combined transport and museum passes. To avoid queuing, prebook integrated passes, or transport, museum and church passes. The sites with the longest queues are St Mark's Basilica, the Doge's Palace and the Accademia. The attractions that must be prebooked are the Clock Tower and the Secret Itineraries tour of the Doge's Palace.

Venezia Unica City Pass (www.veneziaunica.it) is an integrated, online-only booking system for key museums and transport, with discounts offered in quieter periods. The price of a Silver Venezia Unica City Pass starts from €33.90 per adult (museums and churches but no public transport) and a Gold City Pass costs from €78.90 (museums and churches with public transport).

Museum Pass (www.veneziaunica.com) covers 11 civic museums while **Chorus Pass** covers the 16 Chorus Churches (see page 122), all passes are integrated with the Venezia Unica City Pass and can be bought online at www.veneziaunica.it.

Rolling Venice is a youth pass for those aged between 6 and 29. For €6 expect museum discounts, along with a discounted 72-hour *vaporetto* pass for only €22. A €34 version includes a return ticket from/to Marco Polo airport. Buy the pass online at www.veneziaunica.it.

High water. You might just be affected by high water *(acque alte)* in Venice in winter so be prepared. Tidal levels are calculated according to mean water levels at the Punta della Salute, facing St Mark's. When tides above 110cm are forecast, warning sirens wail, while duckboards are erected on key routes and by jetties; wellington boots are needed if tides are over 120cms (4ft), but the ferry *(vaporetto)* service remains operational. The good news is that although High Water follows the tidal cycle, 6 hours up and 6 hours down, very high water usually only lasts 3–4 hours before subsiding.

TRAVELLERS WITH DISABILITIES

With its narrow alleys and stepped bridges, Venice is a challenge, especially if you are not travelling through a specialist tour operator or able to splash out on water taxis. Ideally book through a specialist foreign operator. **Accessible Italy** (tel: 39-378 94 1111; www.accessibleitaly.com) provides a list. For transport tips, see **Venezia Unica** (www.veneziaunica.it) and check the 'Accessible Venice' section. As for hotels, avoid the Santa Croce and San Polo areas, which are unsuitable, and ideally opt for a Grand Canal hotel near a ferry stop. As for walks, ramps along the Zattere make this delightful stroll more accessible. You may also consult www.sagetraveling.com/Venice-Disabled-Access **to find information on accessible Venice. The tourist office** supplies maps marking accessible areas, bridges with ramps for wheelchairs, and toilets for the disabled. Accessible attractions (note that no differentiation is made between full and partial access) include the Basilica San Marco, Palazzo Ducale, Ca' Rezzonico, and the churches of the Frari and La Salute.

V

VISA AND ENTRY REQUIREMENTS

EU citizens: a valid passport or identity card is all that is needed to enter Italy for stays of up to 90 days. Please check for new regulations post-Brexit. Citizens of Australia, Canada, New Zealand and the US require only a valid passport.

Visas. For stays of more than 90 days a visa *(permesso di soggiorno)* or residence permit is required. Regulations change from time to time, so check with the Italian Embassy (www.esteri.it) or in your home country before you travel.

Customs. Free exchange of non-duty-free goods for personal use is allowed between countries within the European Union (EU). Refer to your home country's regulating organisation for a current list of import restrictions.

Currency restrictions. Tourists may bring €10,000 cash (or equivalent in currency) into the country.

W

WEBSITES, APPS AND INTERNET

http://actv.avmspa.it – ACTV Public water transport, maps, ferry routes and timetables

www.veneziaunica.it – the city's official tourism website

http://avm.avmspa.it – AVM Holding Venezia transport website

www.labiennale.org – everything you need to know about this biennial modern art show

www.visitmuve.it – information about Venice's museums

www.jewishvenice.org – information about the Jewish presence in Venice

http://en.turismovenezia.it – the official tourist website of the region

Tap Venice Eating – iPhone app from iTunes (£2.99). Reliable insiders' restaurant guide by local, Michela Scibilia, and tagged by 'best seafood', 'scenic view', etc.

Most good hotels offer internet access (often charged) but a number of budget ones offer it for free. The city-wide **Wi-Fi access scheme** (www.veneziaunica.it/en/content/wi-fi-connection-rolling-venice) costs €5 per day and €20 for a week but check the signal works properly in your chosen spots (there are 200 of them in the area) before buying a package. Venice has few **internet points**, with useful ones being the toyshop on Campo Santa Barnaba, which costs around €8 per hour.

YOUTH HOSTELS

There are several youth hostels (*ostelli della gioventù*) in Venice, with at least three in Giudecca, the best location. Particularly recommended is **Generator Venice** (Fondamenta Zitelle 86, Giudecca; tel: 041-877 8288; http://staygenerator.com).

RECOMMENDED HOTELS

Venice excels at cultural one-upmanship, even in the bedroom. You can sleep in Tchaikovsky's bed or wake up in palaces that welcomed Doges, Henry James and Hemingway. Venetian style swings between grandeur and domesticity. If you hanker after decadence and drama, choose a grand pile on the Grand Canal. If you yearn for a quiet life, chiming bells and secret gardens, slip into a family-owned *palazzo* in the backwaters of Cannaregio. Or, for a sense of stripped-back Venice before the interior decorators moved in, retreat to a bucolic inn on Burano, the lagoon's friendliest island.

Hotels closest to San Marco tend to be pricier but search out midweek or seasonal deals online. Note that the same grand hotel can offer both charming or gloomy rooms so try to change yours if it isn't satisfactory.

The ranges below indicate the price of a double room with bath/shower per night. The nearest *vaporetto* (ferry/waterbus) stop to a hotel is given at the end of each listing.

€€€€   €400 and above
€€€   €280–400
€€   €150–280
€   €150 and under

SAN MARCO

Albergo Hotel San Samuele € *Salizzada San Samuele, tel: 041-520 5165,* www.hotelsansamuele.com. Tucked away behind Palazzo Grassi, this central budget hotel has charming service, provided by a hands-on French owner, sunny, pared-down rooms and free Wi-Fi. It's great value for the arty area and benefits from the services of Venice's only transgender gondolier (http://alexhaigondolatours.com). Vaporetto: San Samuele.

Flora €€€ *Calle dei Bergamaschi, off Calle Larga XXII Marzo, tel: 041-520 5844,* www.hotelflora.it. This is a charming, sought-after, family-run hotel set in a quiet spot near St Mark's. Bedrooms can be palatial or poky (try no. 32 that leads to the garden). Breakfast is in the secluded courtyard garden. Vaporetto: Santa Maria del Giglio.

Gritti Palace €€€€ *Campo Santa Maria del Giglio, tel: 041-794 611*, www. marriott.com. This is the grandest of *grande-dame* hotels: Hemingway, Churchill and Greta Garbo all stayed in this 15th-century palace. The most patrician hotel in Venice, it retains the air of a private *palazzo*, with Murano chandeliers and damask furnishings. Vaporetto: Santa Maria del Giglio.

Luna Baglioni €€€€ *San Marco 1243, tel: 041-528 9840*, www.baglioni hotels.com. The oldest hotel in Venice was originally a Knights Templar lodge for pilgrims en route to Jerusalem. Just off Piazza San Marco, this dowager-style hotel has Venetian decor, an 18th-century ballroom and the grandest breakfast room in Venice. Vaporetto: San Marco-Vallaresso.

Monaco e Grand Canal €€€–€€€€ *Calle Vallaresso, tel: 041-520 0211*, www.hotelmonaco.it. Lap up this mix of slick contemporary and classic Venetian style, with a chic bar and waterfront breakfast room. The hotel's Palazzo Salvadego is more typically Venetian, and less expensive, but shares the same smart breakfast room. Vaporetto: San Marco-Vallaresso.

Novecento €€ *Calle del Dose, San Marco 2683/4, tel: 041-241 3765*, www. novecento.biz. This ethnic-chic boutique hotel offers an exotic touch of Marrakech in Venice, with funky Moroccan lamps and Turkish rugs. The oriental decor extends to the nine individually furnished rooms. Expect beamed ceilings, cosy bedrooms and breakfast in the pretty summer courtyard. The inn is close to San Marco and is owned by the same family as the **Flora**. Vaporetto: Santa Maria del Giglio.

Palazzo del Giglio €€–€€€ *Sestiere, San Marco 2462, tel: 041-852 1091*, www.hotelgiglio.com. This small comfortable hotel overlooking Piazza Santa Maria del Giglio is conveniently located close to St Mark's and La Fenice theatre. Traditional, Venetian-style rooms are fitted with Murano glass lamps and hydromassage tubs. Five rooms and 19 suites. Vaporetto: Santa Maria del Giglio.

CASTELLO

B&B San Marco € *Fondamenta San Giorgio degli Schiavoni, Castello 3385/L, tel: 041-522 7589*, www.realvenice.it. Set on the third floor, this basic but friendly B&B offers rooftop or canal vistas, but it's also about the location, five minutes from St Mark's. Its sister B&B is also featured on the same website. Vaporetto: San Zaccaria.

Danieli €€€€ *Riva degli Schiavoni, Castello 4196, tel: 041-522 6480*, www.marriott.com. Set on the waterfront, this world-famous hotel has a splendid Gothic foyer, and plush rooms with parquet floors and gilded bedsteads; choose the *'casa vecchia'* Doge's residence not the 'Danielino' luxe part. Splendid rooftop restaurant. Vaporetto: San Zaccaria.

Gabrielli €€€ *Riva degli Schiavoni, San Marco, 4110, tel: 041-523 1580*, www.hotelgabrielli.it. Set in a Gothic palace, with great vistas from its rooftop sun terrace, this large hotel has 82 rooms with pleasant, traditional decor, including 27 with lagoon views. In summer, meals are served in a pretty courtyard; there's also a waterfront restaurant, a garden and a panoramic terrace. Vaporetto: San Zaccaria or Arsenale.

La Residenza €–€€ *Campo Bandiera e Moro, Castello 3608, tel: 041-528 5315*, www.venicelaresidenza.com. This pared back yet atmospheric 15th-century palace has unusual public areas. Set on a pleasant square off the tourist trail, the hotel offers just 15 simple but adequate bedrooms – book ahead to ensure one of the best ones. Vaporetto: San Zaccaria or Arsenale.

Liassidi Palace €€€ *Ponte dei Greci 3405, tel: 041-520 5658*, www.liassidipalacehotel.com. Hide out in a boutique hotel in a Gothic palace behind the Riva degli Schiavoni. A muted yet sleek interior embraces individualistic bedrooms in everything from Art Deco to Bauhaus design. There's a bar but no restaurant. Vaporetto: San Zaccaria.

Locanda Casa Querini €€ *Campo San Giovanni Novo, Castello 4388, tel: 041-241 1294*, www.locandaquerini.com. Set close to Campo Santa Maria

Formosa, this small, well-run inn has 11 spacious, low-key rooms, decorated in 17th-century Venetian style. Vaporetto: San Zaccaria or Rialto.

Locanda La Corte €–€€ *Calle Bressana, Castello 6317, tel: 041-241 1300*, www.locandalacorte.it. This is a small Gothic palace off Campo SS Giovanni e Paolo. The decor is a muted version of traditional Venetian style, with an inner courtyard for breakfast. Bedrooms overlook the canal or the courtyard. Vaporetto: Ospedale.

Londra Palace €€€–€€€€ *Riva degli Schiavoni, Castello 4171, tel: 041-520 0533*, www.londrapalace.com. Londra Palace, where Tchaikovsky composed his Fourth Symphony, is a face-lifted *grande-dame*, boasting 100 windows overlooking the lagoon. Here, a room with a view will transform your stay. For drama and waterside bustle, command a fourth-floor window box over the dizzying lagoon. To wallow in wistfulness, hide out under the eaves on the fifth floor, where 502 revels in views across the lagoon to San Giorgio.

Metropole €€€€ *Riva degli Schiavoni 4149, tel: 041-520 5044*, www.hotel metropole.com. This boutique hotel is dotted with eclectic antiques and *objets d'art* It has Met, a Michelin-starred restaurant, a trendy bar, lovely garden courtyard and lagoon or canal views; rooms can be cosy (no. 350) or amusingly kitsch (no. 251). Vaporetto: San Zaccaria.

Palazzo Schiavoni €€ *Fondamenta dei Furlani 3288, tel: 041-241 1275*, www.palazzoschiavoni.com. Expect rooms and apartments in a tastefully converted palace (with the odd frescoed ceiling) beside the Scuola di San Giorgio. This is a good choice for families. Vaporetto: San Zaccaria.

DORSODURO

Accademia Villa Marevege €€ *Fondamenta Bollani 1058, Dorsoduro, tel: 041-521 0188*, www.pensioneaccademia.it. This is a gracious, sought-after wisteria-clad villa at the Grand Canal end of Rio San Trovaso. Expect atmospheric bedrooms and lovely canalside gardens, where breakfast is served in summer, and sunsets are toasted in style. Vaporetto: Accademia.

Bloom/7 Cielo €€ *Campiello Santo Stefano, San Marco 3470, tel: 340-149 8872,* www.bloom-venice.com *and* www.settimocielo-venice.com. Overlooking Campo Santo Stefano, these twin B&Bs are set on the upper floors of a grand *palazzo* but are different in mood. **7 Cielo** (meaning Seventh Heaven) is overtly romantic, with Murano-tiled bathrooms and moody bedrooms. **Bloom** is distinctly Baroque, with bold colours and gilded beds. Vaporetto: Accademia.

Ca' Maria Adele €€€–€€€€ *Rio Terrà Catecumeni, Dorsoduro 111, tel: 041-520 3078,* www.camariaadele.it. Expect Baroque glamour, bohemian charm and canal views in a boutique gem beside La Salute. Eclectic, Oriental and Venetian decor spills over into the themed rooms, such as the Doge's Room, a riot of red brocade, or the Sala dei Mori, which has lovely views. Attentive staff. Vaporetto: Salute.

Ca' Pisani €€–€€€ *Rio Terrà Foscarini, Dorsoduro 979, tel: 041-240 1411,* www.capisanihotel.it. Set in a historic *palazzo* near the Accademia, this is a glamorous, rather retro Art Deco-style retreat, despite Wi-Fi throughout. Other touches include the peaceful patio breakfasts and a stylish wine bar/restaurant. Vaporetto: Accademia or Zattere.

Ca' San Trovaso € *Fondamenta delle Eremite, Dorsoduro 1350/51, tel: 041-241 2215,* www.casantrovaso.com. This unpretentious little hotel on a quiet canal has terracotta floors and damask wallpaper, but no television or telephones in the rooms. Nice roof terrace. Vaporetto: Ca' Rezzonico or San Basilio.

Charming House DD.724 €€€ *Ramo de Mula, Dorsoduro 724, tel: 041-277 0262,* www.thecharminghouse.com. This sleek, modernist-chic designer retreat is for those tired of time-warp *grande-dame* hotels, but is quirky and cosy enough to appeal to old Venetian hands. Also consider **DD.694**, the sister apartment nearby, and a similar retreat in Castello. Vaporetto: Accademia.

Don Orione € *Rio Tera Foscarini, Dorsoduro 909/A, tel: 041-522 4077,* www. donorione-venezia.it. Situated on a chic square near the Accademia, this former orphanage and monastery is now used as a superior hostel run by a religious foundation. The Gothic cloisters and tranquil gardens are open to guests. Expect comfortable rooms, private bathrooms and a restaurant. Vaporetto: Accademia.

La Calcina €€ *Fondamenta Zattere ai Gesuati, Dorsoduro 780, tel: 041-520 6466*, www.lacalcina.com. Overlooking the Giudecca canal, this is a popular, romantic inn, where Victorian art critic John Ruskin lodged in 1876. Enjoy the charming roof terrace and uncluttered bedrooms (try no. 127) plus the waterside La Calcina dining room and terrace. Book early. Vaporetto: Zattere.

Locanda Art Deco €€ *Calle delle Botteghe, 2966, tel: 041-277 0558*, www. locandaartdeco.com. Close to the Accademia, and in charming Art Deco style, the hotel is matched by the Residenza, its sister apartments, which were good enough for Angelina Jolie's babysitters and body-guards. Vaporetto: Sant'Angelo or Accademia.

Locanda San Barnaba €€–€ *Calle del Traghetto, Dorsoduro 2785-2786, tel: 041-241 1233*, www.locanda-sanbarnaba.com. This small inn near Ca' Rezzonico occupies a 16th-century frescoed palace run by the ancestral owner. Expect Venetian-style rooms, including a few with balconies, and a pretty canalside courtyard for breakfast. Vaporetto: Ca' Rezzonico.

SAN POLO, SANTA CROCE AND CANNAREGIO

Abbazia €€ *Calle Priuli dei Cavaletti, Cannaregio 68, tel: 041-717 333*, www. abbaziahotel.com. Set close to the Ca d'Oro, this romantic 16th-century palace features stuccoed salons adorned with School of Tintoretto paintings and Murano chandeliers, matched by frescoed, silk-lined bedrooms and sumptuous tester beds. The moody private residence boasts canalside views and a secret garden. Vaporetto: Ferrovia.

Ai Mori d'Oriente €€–€€€ *Fondamenta della Sensa, Cannaregio 3319, tel: 041-711 001*, www.morihotel.com. This is a quirky boutique hotel near the Ghetto with lots of character and eclectic and exotic touches, plus welcoming staff. Vaporetto: Madonna dell'Orto.

Ca' Sagredo €€€–€€€€ *Campo Santa Sofia 4198/99, Ca' D'Oro, tel: 041-241 3111,* www.casagredohotel.com. Ca' Sagredo occupies a historic Grand Canal *palazzo* adorned with fabulous frescoes by Tiepolo and Sebastiano Ricci. Many rooms have Grand Canal views; you can breakfast under a Tiepolo ceiling or sip cocktails on the canalside bar. The hotel can also provide a babysitter, personal shopper or personal trainer on request. Vaporetto: Ca' d'Oro.

Casa del Melograno € *Campiello del Ponte Storto, Cannaregio 2023, tel: 041-520 8807,* www.locandadelmelograno.it. Tucked away off the busy Strada Nuova shopping street, this guesthouse is a handy budget option, with a private garden, and rooms in a simple modern style. Vaporetto: San Marcuola.

Domus Orsoni €–€€ *Corte Vedei, Cannaregio 1045, tel: 041-275 9538,* www.domusorsoni.it. Set near the Ghetto, this stylish, mosaic-studded guesthouse belongs to a mosaic-producing company with the only furnace allowed to function in central Venice. Enjoy the charming walled garden; try a mosaic course too. Vaporetto: San Marcuola.

Giorgione €€ *Calle Larga dei Proverbi, Cannaregio 4587, tel: 041-522 5810,* www.hotelgiorgione.com. Not far from the Ca' d'Oro, this family-run, 15th-century *palazzo* offers appealing balconies. Decor is traditional Venetian, with chandeliers and Murano glass, the breakfast room opens onto a courtyard; free afternoon coffee and cakes. Vaporetto: Ca' d'Oro.

Grand Hotel Dei Dogi €€€–€€€€ *Fondamenta Madonna dell'Orto (Calle Larga Piave), 3500, tel: 041-220 8111,* www.dahotels.com. This is a grand hotel marooned on the edge of the lagoon. A former monastery, it is still an oasis of calm, with quiet, tasteful Venetian decor and the largest and loveliest hotel garden in Venice. Vaporetto: Madonna dell'Orto; also a courtesy motorboat shuttle.

Palazzo Abadessa €€€ *Calle Priuli, Cannaregio 4011, tel: 041-241 3784,* www.abadessa.com. Tucked away behind Ca d'Oro, this romantic boutique hotel is both patrician and homely, with breakfast amid birdsong in the walled garden. The stuccoed salons are adorned with School of

Tintoretto art and Murano chandeliers, matched by frescoed, silk-lined bedrooms and sumptuous tester beds. Best bedrooms are the junior suites (23 and 21). Vaporetto: Ca' d'Oro.

3749 Ponte Chiodo € *Ponte Chiodo, Cannaregio 3749, tel: 041-241 3935, www.pontechiodo.it.* Located in the Cannaregio backwaters, this is a budget guesthouse with rare amenities such as Wi-Fi and air conditioning. The friendly owner may eat breakfast with his guests and provide valuable information about the city. Vaporetto: Ca' d'Oro.

GIUDECCA

Bauer Palladio Hotel & Spa €€€–€€€€ *Fondamenta della Croce, Isola della Giudecca, S. Marco 1459, tel: 041-520 7022, www.bauervenezia. com.* Set in Palladio-designed cloisters, this serene, somewhat austere space has garden terraces, canalside views and a special spa, a luxury villa next-door and a courtesy shuttle boat to the more worldly Bauers over the water. Vaporetto: Zitelle.

Belmond Cipriani €€€€ *Isola della Giudecca 10, tel: 041-240 801/0185 2678 451, www.belmond.com/hotel-cipriani-venice.* Beloved by movie stars, the Belmond Cipriani can be seen as a cliché, but it conveys a sense of warmth and intimacy better than most other grand hotels. Vaporetto: Zitelle (and a complimentary motor launch to St Mark's).

Casa Genoveffa €–€€ *Calle del Forno, 472, Giudecca, tel: 347-250 7809, www.casagenoveffa.com.* Tucked away down a back alley, this unpretentious but cosy B&B has beamed rooms and four-poster beds. Vaporetto: Palanca.

Hilton Molino Stucky €€€ *Isola della Giudecca 810, tel: 041-272 3311, www3.hilton.com;* good deals online. This formidable-looking flour mill on the Giudecca waterfront is now a luxury hotel with a rooftop pool, magical terrace, great views and the cool Skyline rooftop bar. A spa, several restaurants and a ground-floor bar add to the holiday feel. Vaporetto: Palanca (and a complimentary shuttle boat to St Mark's).

THE LIDO, MURANO, BURANO AND TORCELLO

Locanda Cipriani €€ *Piazza Santa Fosca 29, Isola di Torcello, tel: 041-730 150*, www.locandacipriani.com. This bucolic inn beloved by Hemingway is set in a seemingly remote spot. Run by a branch of the Cipriani family, the inn boasts a celebrated homely restaurant, with a garden for outdoor dining. Vaporetto from Fondamenta Nuove to Torcello.

Murano Palace €–€€ *Fondamenta Vetrai 77, Isola di Murano, tel: 041-739 655*, www.muranopalace.com. Set on Murano, this is a rewarding, underpriced gem, with splendid Murano chandeliers and canal views. It is eerily quiet after the glass-shoppers go home, but compensations lie in the lagoon pursuits, such as sailing, rowing and fishing, and the family's restaurant nearby. There are also plenty of ferries to whisk you back to central Venice. Vaporetto from Fondamenta Nuove to Colonna stop (Murano).

Rivamare €–€€ *Lungomare Marconi 44, Lido, tel: 041-526 0352*, www.hotelrivamare.com. This welcoming, family-run beach hotel is perfect for young families. Some rooms have sea views and small balconies and there's a summer terrace. Rivamare also works for seekers (separately run meditation and Reiki centre). Vaporetto: Lido.

Venissa €€ *Fondamenta Santa Caterina 3, Isola di Mazzorbo (Burano), tel: 041-527 2281*, www.venissa.it. Run by the Bisol Prosecco dynasty, this quaint island guesthouse, gourmet restaurant and wine estate revels in creative cuisine. The guesthouse and restaurant are both closed in winter. Vaporetto: ferry 41/42 from Fondamenta Nuove to Mazzorbo, then cross the footbridge.

DICTIONARY

ENGLISH–ITALIAN

adj adjective   **adv** adverb   **BE** British English   **n** noun   **prep** preposition   **v** verb

A

a.m. del mattino
abbey l'abbazia
accept v accettare
access l'accesso
accident l'incidente
accommodation
   l'alloggio
account il conto
acupuncture
   l'agopuntura
adapter l'adattatore
address l'indirizzo
admission l'ingresso
after dopo; **~noon** il
   pomeriggio; **~shave**
   il dopobarba
age l'età
agency l'agenzia
AIDS l'AIDS
air l'aria; **~ condition-**
   ing l'aria condizionata; **~ pump** la
   pompa dell'aria; **~line**
   la compagnia aerea;
   ~mail la posta aerea;
   ~plane l'aereo;
   ~port l'aeroporto
aisle il corridoio; **~ seat**
   il posto sul corridoio
allergic allergico; **~**
   reaction la reazione
   allergica

allow v permettere
alone solo
alter v modificare
alternate route il
   percorso alternativo
aluminum foil la carta
   stagnola
amazing straordinario
ambulance
   l'ambulanza
American americano
amusement park il
   lunapark
and and
anemic anemico
anesthesia l'anestesia
animal l'animale
ankle la caviglia
antibiotic l'antibiotico
antiques store il
   negozio d'antiquariato
antiseptic cream la
   crema antisettica
anything qualsiasi
   cosa
apartment
   l'appartamento
appendix (body part)
   l'appendice
appetizer l'antipasto
appointment
   l'appuntamento
arcade la sala giochi

area code il prefisso
arm il braccio
aromatherapy
   l'aromaterapia
around (the corner)
   dietro di
arrivals (airport) gli
   arrivi
arrive v arrivare
artery l'arteria
arthritis l'artrite
art l'arte
aspirin l'aspirina
asthmatic asmatico
ATM il bancomat
attack l'aggressione
attend v frequentare
attraction (place)
   l'attrattiva
attractive attraente
Australia Australia
Australian australiano
automatic automatico;
   ~ car l'auto col
   cambio automatico
available libero

B

baby il bebè; **~ bottle**
   il biberon; **~ wipe** la
   salvietta per neonati;
   ~sitter la babysitter
back (body part) la

schiena; **~ache** il
   mal di schiena;
   ~pack lo zaino
bag la borsa
baggage il bagaglio;
   ~ claim il ritiro
   bagagli; **~ ticket** lo
   scontrino bagagli
bakery la panetteria
ballet lo spettacolo
   di danza
bandage la benda
bank la banca
bar il bar
barbecue il barbecue
barber il barbiere
baseball il baseball
basket (grocery store)
   il cestino
basketball il
   basketball
bathroom il bagno
battery la batteria
battleground il campo
   di battaglia
be v essere
beach la spiaggia
beautiful bello
bed il letto; **~**
   and breakfast
   la pensione
begin v iniziare
before prima

beginner il principiante

behind dietro

beige beige

belt la cintura

berth la cuccetta

best il migliore

better migliore

bicycle la bicicletta

big grande

bigger più grande

bike route il percorso ciclabile

bikini il bikini; ~ **wax** la ceretta all'inguine

bill v (charge) fatturare; ~ n (money) la banconota; ~ n (of sale) il conto

bird l'uccello

birthday il compleanno

black nero

bladder la vescica

bland insipido

blanket la coperta

bleed v sanguinare

blood il sangue; ~ **pressure** la pressione sanguigna

blouse la camicetta

blue blu

board v imbarcarsi

boarding pass la carta d'imbarco

boat la barca

bone l'osso

book il libro; ~**store** la libreria

boots gli stivali

boring noioso

botanical garden il giardino botanico

bother v infastidire

bottle la bottiglia; ~ **opener** l'apribottiglie

bowl la coppa

box la scatola

boxing match l'incontro di boxe

boy il ragazzo; ~**friend** il ragazzo

bra il reggiseno

bracelet il braccialetto

brakes (car) i freni

break v rompere; ~-**in (burglary)** il furto con scasso; ~**down** il guasto

breakfast la colazione

breast il petto; ~**feed** v allattare

breathe v respirare

bridge il ponte

briefs (clothing) lo slip

bring v portare

British britannico(a)

broken rotto

brooch la spilla

broom la scopa

brother il fratello

brown marrone

bug l'insetto

building l'edificio

burn v bruciare

bus l'autobus; ~ **station** la stazione degli autobus; ~ **stop** la fermata del bus; ~ **ticket** il biglietto del bus; ~ **tour** l'escursione in pullman

business il lavoro; ~ **card** il biglietto da visita; ~ **center** il centro business; ~ **class** la classe business; ~ **hours** l'orario d'apertura

butcher il macellaio

buttocks le natiche

buy v comprare

bye ciao

C

cabaret il cabaret

cabin la cabina

cable car la funivia

cafe il caffè

call v chiamare; ~ n la chiamata

calories le calorie

camera la macchina fotografica; **digital ~** la macchina fotografica digitale; ~ **case** l'astuccio della macchina fotografica; ~ **store** il negozio di fotografia

camp v campeggiare; ~ **stove** il fornello da campeggio; ~**site** il campeggio

can opener l'apriscatole

Canada il Canada

Canadian canadese

cancel v annullare

candy le caramelle

canned good lo scatolame

canyon il canalone

car l'auto; ~ **hire**

[BE] l'autonoleggio; ~ **park [BE]** il parcheggio; ~ **rental** l'autonoleggio; ~ **seat** il seggiolino per auto

carafe la caraffa

card la carta; **ATM ~** il bancomat; **credit ~** la carta di credito; **debit ~** il bancomat; **phone ~** la scheda telefonica

carry on board v [BE] portare a bordo

carry-on il bagaglio a mano

cart (grocery store) il carrello; ~ **(luggage)** il carrello

carton il cartone; ~ **of cigarettes** la stecca di sigarette

case (container) la cassa

cash v incassare; ~ n i contanti; ~ **advance** l'acconto

cashier il cassiere

casino il casinò

castle il castello

cathedral la cattedrale

cave la grotta

CD il CD

cell phone il telefonino

Celsius Celsius

centimeter il centimetro

certificate il certificato

chair la sedia; **~ lift** la seggiovia

change v (buses) cambiare; ~ v (money) cambiare; ~ v (baby) cambiare; ~ n (money) il cambio

charcoal il carbone

charge v (credit card) addebitare; ~ n (cost) il costo

cheap economico; **~er** più economico

check v (on something) controllare; ~ v (luggage) controllare; ~ n (payment) l'assegno; **~-in (hotel/airport)** il check-in; **~ing account** il conto corrente; **~-out (hotel)** il pagamento del conto

Cheers! Salute!

chemical toilet il WC da campeggio

chemist [BE] la farmacia

cheque [BE] l'assegno

chest (body part) il petto; **~ pain** il dolore al petto

chewing gum la gomma da masticare

child il bambino; **~ seat** il seggiolone; **~'s menu** il menù per bambino; **~'s portion** la porzione per bambino

Chinese cinese

chopsticks i bastoncini cinesi

church la chiesa

cigar il sigaro

cigarette la sigaretta

class la classe; **business ~** la classe business; **economy ~** la classe economica; **first ~** la prima classe

classical music la musica classica

clean v pulire; ~ adj pulito; **~ing product** il prodotto per la pulizia; **~ing supplies** i prodotti per la pulizia

clear v (on an ATM) cancellare

cliff la scogliera

cling film [BE] la pellicola per alimenti

close v (a shop) chiudere

close vicino

closed chiuso

clothing l'abbigliamento; **~ store** il negozio d'abbigliamento

club il club

coat il cappotto

coffee shop il caffè

coin la moneta

colander la scolapasta

cold (sickness) il raffreddore; ~ (temperature) freddo

colleague il collega

cologne la colonia

color il colore

comb il pettine

come v venire

complaint il reclamo

computer il computer

concert il concerto; **~ hall** la sala da concerti

condition (medical) la condizione

conditioner il balsamo

condom il preservativo

conference la conferenza

confirm v confermare

congestion la congestione

connect v (internet) collegarsi

connection (internet) il collegamento; ~ (flight) la coincidenza

constipated costipato

consulate il consolato

consultant il consulente

contact v contattare; **~ lens** la lente a contatto; **~ lens solution** la soluzione per lenti a contatto

contagious contagioso

convention hall la sala congressi

conveyor belt il nastro trasportatore

cook v cucinare

cooking gas il gas per cucina

cool (temperature) fresco

copper il rame

corkscrew il cavatappi

cost v costare

cot il lettino

cotton il cotone

cough v tossire; ~ n la tosse

country code il prefisso del paese

cover charge il coperto

crash v (car) fare un incidente

cream (ointment) la crema

credit card la carta di credito

crew neck a girocollo

crib la culla

crystal il cristallo

cup la tazza

currency la valuta; **~ exchange** il cambio valuta; **~ exchange office** l'ufficio di cambio

current account [BE] il conto corrente

customs la dogana

cut v (hair) tagliare; ~ n (injury) il taglio

cute carino

cycling il ciclismo

D

damage v danneggiare; **~d** danneggiato

dance v ballare; **~ club** il club di ballo; **~ing** il ballo

dangerous pericoloso

dark scuro

date (calendar) la data

day il giorno

deaf sordo

debit card il bancomat

deck chair la sedia a sdraio

declare v dichiarare

decline v (credit card) rifiutare

deeply profondamente

degrees (temperature) i gradi

delay v ritardare

delete v (computer) eliminare

delicatessen la gastronomia

delicious squisito

denim i jeans

dentist il dentista

denture la dentiera

deodorant il deodorante

department store il grande magazzino

departures (airport) le partenze

deposit v depositare; ~ **(bank)** n il deposito; ~ **(to reserve a room)** il deposito

desert il deserto

detergent il detersivo

develop v (film) sviluppare

diabetic diabetico

dial v comporre il numero

diamond il diamante

diaper il pannolino

diarrhea la diarrea

diesel il diesel

difficult difficile

digital digitale; ~ **camera** la macchina fotografica digitale; ~ **photos** le foto digitali; ~ **prints** le stampe digitali

dining room la sala da pranzo

dinner la cena

direction la direzione

dirty sporco

disabled il disabile; ~ **accessible [BE]** accessibile ai disabili

disconnect v (computer) scollegare

discount lo sconto

dish (kitchen) il piatto; ~**washer** la lavastoviglie; ~**washing liquid** il detersivo per i piatti

display lo schermo; ~ **case** la vetrinetta

disposable usa e getta; ~ **razor** la lametta usa e getta

dive v tuffarsi; ~**ing equipment** l'attrezzatura subacquea

divorce v divorziare

dizzy stordito

doctor il medico

doll la bambola

dollar (U.S.) il dollaro

domestic domestico; ~ **flight** il volo nazionale

door la porta

dormitory il dormitorio

double bed il letto matrimoniale

downtown (direction) il centro; ~ **area** il centro

dozen la dozzina

drag lift lo ski lift

dress (piece of clothing) il vestito; ~ **code** il codice di abbigliamento

drink v bere; ~ n la bevanda, ~ **menu** il menù delle bevande; ~**ing water** l'acqua potabile

drive v guidare

driver's license number il numero di patente

drop (medicine) la goccia

drowsiness la sonnolenza

dry cleaner il lavasecco

dubbed doppiato

during durante

duty (tax) la tassa; ~ **free** duty free

DVD il DVD

E

ear l'orecchio; ~**ache** il mal d'orecchio

earlier prima

early presto

earrings gli orecchini

east est

easy facile

eat v mangiare

economy class la classe economica

elbow il gomito

electric outlet la presa elettrica

elevator l'ascensore

e-mail v inviare e-mail; ~ n l'e-mail; ~ **address** l'indirizzo e-mail

emergency l'emergenza; ~ **exit** l'uscita d'emergenza

empty v svuotare

enamel (jewelry) lo smalto

end v finire

English inglese

engrave v incidere

enjoy v godersi

enter v entrare

entertainment l'intrattenimento

entrance l'entrata

envelope la busta

equipment l'attrezzatura

escalators le scale mobili

estate car [BE] la station wagon

e-ticket il biglietto elettronico

EU resident il residente UE

euro l'euro

evening la sera

excess l'eccesso

exchange v (money) cambiare; ~ n **(place)** il cambio; ~ **rate** il tasso di cambio

excursion l'escursione

excuse v scusare

exhausted esausto

exit v uscire; ~ n l'uscita

expensive caro

expert esperto

exposure (film) la posa

express espresso; ~ **bus** il bus espresso; ~ **train** il treno espresso

extension (phone) l'interno

extra extra; ~ **large** extra large

extract v **(tooth)** estrarre

eye l'occhio

eyebrow wax la ceretta per sopracciglie

F

face il viso

facial la pulizia del viso

family la famiglia

fan (appliance) il ventilatore; ~ **(sou-venir)** il ventaglio

far lontano; ~**-sighted** ipermetrope

farm la fattoria

fast veloce; ~ **food** il fast food

faster più veloce

fat free senza grassi

father il padre

fax v inviare per fax; ~ n il fax; ~ **number** il numero di fax

fee la tariffa

feed v dare da mangiare

ferry il traghetto

fever la febbre

field (sports) il campo

fill v riempire; ~ **out** v **(form)** compilare; ~**ing (tooth)** l'otturazione

film (camera) il rullino

fine (fee for breaking law) la multa

finger il dito; ~**nail** l'unghia

fire il fuoco; ~ **department** i vigili del fuoco; ~ **door** la porta antincendio

first primo; ~ **class** la prima classe

fit (clothing) v andare bene

fitting room il camerino

fix v **(repair)** riparare

flashlight la torcia elettrica

flat tire la gomma a terra

flight il volo

floor il pavimento

flower il fiore

folk music la musica folk

food il cibo

foot il piede

football game [BE] la partita di football

for per

forecast la previsione

forest il bosco

fork la forchetta

form il modulo

formula (baby) il latte in polvere

fort la fortezza

fountain la fontana

free libero

freezer il freezer

fresh fresco

friend l'amico

frying pan la padella

full-service il servizio completo

full-time a tempo pieno

G

game la partita

garage il garage

garbage bag il sacchetto per la spazzatura

gas (cooking) il gas per cucina; ~ **(heating)** il gas; ~ **station** la stazione del servizio; ~ **(vehicle)** la benzina

gate (airport) l'uscita

gay gay; ~ **bar** il bar per gay; ~ **club** il club per gay

gel (hair) il gel

get off v **(a train/bus/subway)** scendere

get to v arrivare

gift il regalo; ~ **shop** il negozio di articoli da regalo

girl la ragazza; ~**friend** la ragazza

give v dare

glass (drinking) il bicchiere; ~ **(material)** il vetro; ~**es** gli occhiali

go v **(somewhere)** andare

gold l'oro

golf golf; ~ **course** il campo da golf; ~ **club** la mazza; ~ **tournament** la gara di golf

good n il bene; ~ adj buono; ~ **afternoon** buon pomeriggio; ~ **evening** buonasera; ~ **morning** buongiorno; ~ **bye** arrivederla; ~**s** le merci

gram il grammo

grandchild il nipote

grandparent il nonno

gray grigio

green verde

grocery store il fruttivendolo

ground floor il pianterreno

groundcloth [ground-sheet BE] il telone impermeabile
group il gruppo
guide la guida; **~ book** la guida; **~ dog** il cane da guida
gym la palestra
gynecologist il ginecologo

H

hair i capelli; **~ dryer** l'asciugacapelli; **~ salon** il parrucchiere; **~brush** la spazzola; **~ cut** il taglio; **~spray** la lacca; **~style** l'acconciatura; **~stylist** il parrucchiere
half la metà; **~ hour** la mezz'ora; **~-kilo** il mezzo chilo
hammer il martello
hand la mano; **~ luggage** il bagaglio a mano; **~bag** la borsetta
handicapped il disabile; **~ accessible** accessibile ai disabili
hangover la sbornia
happy felice
hat il cappello
have v avere
head (body part) la testa; **~ache** il mal di testa; **~phones** gli auricolari
health la salute; **~ food store**

l'erboristeria
heart il cuore; **~ condition** il disturbo cardiaco
heat il calore; **~er** il radiatore
hello salve
helmet il casco
help v aiutare; **~** n l'aiuto
here qui
heterosexual eterosessuale
hi ciao
high alto; **~chair** il seggiolone; **~-heeled shoes** le scarpe col tacco alto; **~way** l'autostrada
hiking boots gli scarponi da montagna
hill la collina
hire v [BE] noleggiare; **~ car [BE]** l'auto a noleggio
hitchhike v fare l'autostop
hockey l'hockey
holiday [BE] la vacanza
horse track l'ippodromo
hospital l'ospedale
hostel l'ostello
hot (temperature) caldo; **~ (spicy)** piccante; **~ springs** le terme; **~ water** l'acqua calda
hotel l'hotel
hour l'ora
house la casa; **~hold**

goods gli articoli casalinghi; **~keeping services** i servizi di pulizia domestica
how come; **~ much** quanto
hug v abbracciare
hungry affamato
hurt il dolore
husband il marito

I

ibuprofen l'ibuprofene
ice il ghiaccio; **~ hockey** l'hockey su ghiaccio
icy gelato
identification l'identificazione
ill malato
in in
include v includere
indoor pool la piscina interna
inexpensive a buon mercato
infected infetto
information (phone) le informazioni; **~ desk** l'ufficio informazioni
insect insetto; **~ bite** la puntura d'insetto; **~ repellent** il repellente per gli insetti
insert v inserire
insomnia l'insonnia
instant message il messaggio istantaneo
insulin l'insulina
insurance l'assicurazione;

~ card la tessera dell'assicurazione; **~ company** la compagnia di assicurazione
interesting interessante
intermediate intermedio
international (airport area) internazionale; **~ flight** il volo internazionale; **~ student card** la tessera internazionale dello studente
internet l'Internet; **~ cafe** l'Internet caffè; **~ service** il servizio Internet; **wireless ~** il collegamento wireless a Internet
interpreter l'interprete
intersection l'incrocio
intestine l'intestino
introduce v presentare
invoice [BE] la fattura
Ireland l'Irlanda
Irish irlandese
iron v stirare; **~** n **(clothes)** il ferro da stiro
Italian italiano
Italy l'Italia

J

jacket la giacca
jar il vaso
jaw la mascella
jazz il jazz; **~ club** il club jazz
jeans i jeans

jet ski l'acquascooter
jeweler il gioielliere
jewelry la gioielleria
join v unire
joint (body part) la giuntura

K

key la chiave; **~ card** la chiave elettronica; **~ ring** il portachiavi
kiddie pool la piscina per bambini
kidney (body part) il rene
kilo il chilo; **~gram** il chilogrammo; **~meter** il chilometro
kiss v baciare
kitchen la cucina; **~ foil** la carta stagnola
knee il ginocchio
knife il coltello

L

lace il pizzo
lactose intolerant intollerante al lattosio
lake il lago
large grande
larger più grande
last ultimo
late (time) tardi
later più tardi
launderette [BE] la lavanderia a gettone
laundromat la lavanderia a gettone
laundry la lavanderia; **~ facility** il locale

lavanderia; **~ service** il servizio di lavanderia
lawyer l'avvocato
leather la pelle
leave v partire
left (direction) a sinistra
leg la gamba
lens la lente
less meno
lesson la lezione
letter la lettera
library la biblioteca
life la vita; **~ jacket** il giubbotto di salvataggio; **~guard** il bagnino
lift (ride) il passaggio; **~ [BE]** l'ascensore; **~ pass** il lift pass
light (overhead) la lampada; **~** v **(cigarette)** accendere; **~bulb** la lampadina; **~er** l'accendino
like v **(someone)** piacere
line (train) la linea
linen il lino
lip il labbro
liquor store l'enoteca
liter il litro
little piccolo
live v vivere
liver (body part) il fegato
loafers i mocassini
local locale
lock v chiudere; **~** n la serratura
locker l'armadietto

log off v **(computer)** fare il logoff
log on v **(computer)** fare il logon
long lungo; **~ sleeves** le maniche lunghe; **~-sighted [BE]** ipermetrope
look v guardare
lose v **(something)** perdere
lost perso; **~ and found** l'ufficio oggetti smarriti
lotion la lozione
louder più forte
love v **(someone)** amare; **~** n l'amore
low basso; **~er** più basso
luggage il bagaglio; **~ cart** il carrello bagagli; **~ locker** l'armadietto dei bagagli; **~ ticket** lo scontrino dei bagagli; **hand ~ [BE]** il bagaglio a mano
lunch il pranzo
lung il polmone

M

magazine la rivista
magnificent magnifico
mail v spedire; **~** n la posta; **~box** la cassetta della posta
main principale; **~ attraction** l'attrattiva principale; **~ course** il piatto principale
make up [BE] (a prescription) il trucco
mall il centro commerciale
man l'uomo
manager il responsabile
manicure il manicure
manual car l'auto col cambio manuale
map la cartina
market il mercato
married sposato
marry v sposare
mass (church service) la messa
massage il massaggio
match n **(wooden stick)** il fiammifero; **~** n **(game)** la partita
meal il pasto
measure v **(someone/something)** misurare; **~ing cup** la tazza di misurazione; **~ing spoon** il misurino
mechanic il meccanico
medicine la medicina
medium (size) medio
meet v **(someone)** incontrare
meeting (corporate) la riunione; **~ room** sala riunioni
membership card la tessera associativa
memorial (place) il monumento
memory card la scheda memoria

mend v riparare

menstrual cramp il crampo mestruale

menu il menù

message il messaggio

meter (parking) il parchimetro

microwave il microonde

midday [BE] mezzogiorno

midnight mezzanotte

mileage il chilometraggio

mini-bar il minibar

minute il minuto

missing (was never there) mancante; scomparso **(was previously there)**

mistake l'errore

mobile mobile; **~ home** la casa prefabbricata; **~ phone [BE]** il telefonino

mobility la mobilità

money il denaro

month il mese

mop lo spazzolone

moped lo scooter

more più

morning il mattino

mosque la moschea

mother la madre

motor il motore; **~ boat** il motoscafo; **~cycle** la motocicletta; **~way [BE]** l'autostrada

mountain la montagna; **~ bike** la mountain bike

mousse (hair) la mousse

mouth la bocca

movie il film; **~ theater** il cinema

mug v scippare

muscle il muscolo

museum il museo

music la musica; **~ store** il negozio di musica

N

nail l'unghia; **~ file** la lima; **~ salon** il salone di bellezza

name il nome

napkin il tovagliolo

nappy [BE] il pannolino

nationality la nazionalità

nature preserve la riserva naturale

(be) nauseous v avere la nausea

near vicino; **~-sighted** miope

neck il collo; **~lace** la collana

need v necessitare

newspaper il giornale

newsstand l'edicola

next prossimo

nice sympatico

night la notte; **~club** il nightclub

no no

non-alcoholic analcolico

non-smoking non fumatori

noon mezzogiorno

north nord

nose il naso

notes [BE] le banconote

nothing niente

notify v avvertire

novice il principiante

now ora

number il numero

nurse l'infermiere

O

office l'ufficio; **~ hours** l'orario d'ufficio

off-licence [BE] l'enoteca

oil l'olio

OK OK

old vecchio

on the corner all'angolo

once una volta

one uno; **~-way (ticket)** solo andata; **~-way street** il senso unico

only solo

open v aprire; **~** adj aperto

opera l'opera; **~ house** il teatro dell'opera

opposite di fronte a

optician l'ottico

orange (color) arancione

orchestra l'orchestra

order v ordinare

outdoor pool la piscina esterna

outside fuori

over sopra; **~ the counter (medication)** da banco; **~look (scenic place)** il belvedere; **~night** per la notte

oxygen treatment l'ossigeno terapia

P

p.m. del pomeriggio

pacifier il ciuccio

pack v fare le valigie

package il pacchetto

paddling pool [BE] la piscina per bambini

pad [BE] l'assorbente

pain il dolore

pajamas il pigiama

palace il palazzo

pants i pantaloni

pantyhose il collant

paper la carta; **~ towel** la carta da cucina

paracetamol [BE] il paracetamolo

park v parcheggiare; **~** n il parco; **~ing garage** il parcheggio; **~ing lot** il parcheggio

parliament building l'edificio del parlamento

part (for car) il ricambio; **~ time** part-time

pass through v passare

passenger il passeggero

passport il passaporto; **~ control** il controllo passaporti
password la password
pastry shop la pasticceria
path il sentiero
pay *v* pagare; **~ phone** il telefono pubblico
peak (of a mountain) la vetta
pearl la perla
pedestrian il pedone
pediatrician il pediatra
pedicure il pedicure
pen la penna
penicillin la penicillina
per per; **~ day** al giorno; **~ hour** all'ora; **~ night** a notte; **~ week** a settimana
perfume il profumo
period (menstrual) il ciclo; **~ (of time)** il periodo
permit *v* permettere
petite piccolo
petrol [BE] la benzina; **~ station [BE]** la stazione di servizio
pewter il peltro
pharmacy la farmacia
phone *v* telefonare; **~** *n* il telefono; **~ call** la telefonata; **~ card** la scheda telefonica; **~ number** il numero di telefono
photo la foto; **~copy**

la fotocopia; **~graphy** la fotografia
pick up *v* **(something)** raccogliere
picnic area la zona picnic
piece il pezzo
Pill (birth control) la pillola
pillow il cuscino
personal identification number (PIN) il codice PIN
pink rosa
piste [BE] la pista; **~ map [BE]** la cartina delle piste
pizzeria la pizzeria
place a bet *v* scommettere
plane l'aereo
plastic wrap la pellicola per alimenti
plate il piatto
platform (train) il binario
platinum il platino
play *v* giocare; **~** *n* **(theater)** lo spettacolo; **~ ground** il parco giochi; **~ pen** il box
please per favore
pleasure il piacere
plunger lo sturalavandini
plus size la taglia forte
pocket la tasca
poison il veleno
poles (skiing) le racchette

police la polizia; **~ report** il verbale di polizia; **~ station** il commissariato
pond lo stagno
pool (swimming) la piscina
pop music la musica pop
portion la porzione
post [BE] la posta; **~ office** l'ufficio postale; **~box [BE]** la buca delle lettere; **~card** la cartolina
pot (for cooking) la pentola; **~ (for flowers)** il vaso
pottery la ceramica
pounds (British sterling) le sterline
pregnant incinta
prescribe *v* prescrivere
prescription la ricetta
press *v* **(clothing)** stirare
price il prezzo
print *v* stampare
problem il problema
produce la frutta e verdura; **~ store** il fruttivendolo
prohibit *v* proibire
pronounce *v* pronunciare
public pubblico
pull *v* **(door sign)** tirare
purple viola
purse la borsetta
push *v* **(door sign)** spingere; **~chair**

[BE] il passeggino

Q

quality la qualità
question la domanda
quiet tranquillo

R

racetrack il circuito
racket (sports) la racchetta
railway station [BE] la stazione ferroviaria
rain la pioggia; **~coat** l'impermeabile; **~forest** la foresta pluviale; **~y** piovoso
rape *v* stuprare; **~** *n* lo stupro
rash l'irritazione
razor blade la lametta
reach *v* raggiungere
ready pronto
real vero
receipt la ricevuta
receive *v* ricevere
reception la reception
recharge *v* ricaricare
recommend *v* raccomandare
recommendation la raccomandazione
recycling il riciclaggio
red rosso
refrigerator il frigorifero
region la regione
registered mail la raccomandata
regular normale
relationship la relazione

rent *v* affittare

rental car l'auto a noleggio

repair *v* riparare

repeat *v* ripetere

reservation la prenotazione; **~ desk** l'ufficio prenotazioni

reserve *v* prenotare

restaurant il ristorante

restroom la toilette

retired in pensione

return *v* **(something)** portare indietro; **~** *n* **[BE]** la resa

rib (body part) la costola

right (direction) a destra; **~ of way** la precedenza

ring l'anello

river il fiume

road map la cartina stradale

rob *v* rubare; **~bed** derubato

romantic romantico

room la stanza; **~ key** la chiave della stanza; **~ service** il servizio in camera

round-trip l'andata e ritorno

route il percorso

rowboat la barca a remi

rubbish [BE] la spazzatura; **~ bag [BE]** il sacchetto per la spazzatura

rugby il rugby

ruins le rovine

rush la fretta

S

sad triste

safe (receptacle) la cassaforte; **~ (protected)** sicuro

sales tax l'IVA

same stesso

sandals i sandali

sanitary napkin l'assorbente

saucepan la pentola

sauna la sauna

save *v* **(computer)** salvare

savings (account) i risparmi

scanner lo scanner

scarf la sciarpa

schedule *v* programmare; **~** *n* il programma

school la scuola

science la scienza

scissors le forbici

sea il mare

seat il posto

security la sicurezza

see *v* vedere

self-service il self-service

sell *v* vendere

seminar il seminario

send *v* inviare

senior citizen l'anziano

separated (marriage) separato

serious serio

service (in a restaurant) il servizio

sexually transmitted disease (STD) la malattia sessualmente trasmissibile

shampoo lo shampoo

sharp appuntito

shaving cream la crema da barba

sheet (bedlinen) il lenzuolo; **~ (paper)** la pagina

ship *v* **(mail)** inviare

shirt la camicia

shoes le scarpe; **~ store** il negozio di calzature

shop *v* fare lo shopping

shopping lo shopping; **~ area** la zona commerciale; **~ centre [BE]** il centro commerciale; **~ mall** il centro commerciale

short corto; **~ sleeves** le maniche corte; **~s** i pantaloncini corti; **~-sighted [BE]** miope

shoulder la spalla

show *v* mostrare

shower la doccia

shrine il santuario

sick malato

side il lato; **~ dish** il contorno; **~ effect** l'effetto collaterale; **~ order** il contorno

sightseeing la visita turistica; **~ tour** la gita turistica

sign *v* firmare

silk la seta

silver l'argento

single (marriage) single; **~ bed** il letto a una piazza; **~ prints** le stampe singole; **~ room** la stanza singola

sink il lavandino

sister la sorella

sit *v* sedersi

size la taglia

skin la pelle

skirt la gonna

ski *v* sciare; **~** *n* lo sci; **~ lift** lo ski lift

sleep *v* dormire; **~er car** il vagone letto; **~ing bag** il sacco a pelo; **~ing car [BE]** il vagone letto

slice (of something) la fetta

slippers le ciabatte

slow lento; **~er** più lento; **~ly** lentamente

small piccolo; **~er** più piccolo

smoke *v* fumare

smoking (area) per fumatori

snack bar lo snack bar

sneakers le scarpe da ginnastica

snorkeling equipment l'attrezzatura da immersione

snow neve; **~board** lo snowboard; **~shoe** la scarpa da neve; **~y** nevoso

soap il sapone

soccer il calcio

sock il calzino

some qualche

soother [BE] il ciuccio

sore throat il mal di gola

sorry scusi

south sud

souvenir il souvenir; **~ store** il negozio di souvenir

spa la stazione termale

spatula la spatola

speak v parlare

special (food) la specialità; **~ist (doctor)** lo specialista

specimen il campione

speeding l'eccesso di velocità

spell v scrivere

spicy piccante

spine (body part) la spina dorsale

spoon il cucchiaio

sport lo sport; **~s massage** il massaggio sportivo

sporting goods store il negozio di articoli sportivi

sprain la storta

square quadrato; **~ kilometer** il chilometro quadrato; **~ meter** il metro quadrato

stadium lo stadio

stairs le scale

stamp v **(a ticket)** convalidare; **~** n **(postage)** il francobollo

start v iniziare

starter [BE] lo starter

station la stazione; **bus ~** la stazione dei bus; **gas ~** il benzinaio; **petrol ~ [BE]** il benzinaio; **railway ~ [BE]** la stazione ferroviaria; **subway ~** la stazione della metropolitana **train ~** la stazione ferroviaria; **underground ~ [BE]** la stazione della metropolitana; **~ wagon** la station wagon

statue la statua

stay v stare

steal v rubare

steep ripido

sterling silver l'argento massiccio

sting la puntura

stolen rubato

stomach lo stomaco; **~ache** il mal di stomaco

stop v fermarsi; **~** n la fermata

store directory la piantina del negozio

storey [BE] il piano

stove la cucina

straight dritto

strange strano

stream il ruscello

stroller il passeggino

student lo studente

study v studiare

stunning fenomenale

subtitle il sottotitolo

subway la metropolitana; **~ station** la stazione della metropolitana

suit l'abito; **~case** la valigia

sun il sole; **~block** il filtro solare; **~burn** la scottatura; **~glasses** gli occhiali da sole; **~ny** soleggiato; **~screen** il filtro solare; **~stroke** l'insolazione

super (fuel) il super; **~market** il supermercato; **~vision** la supervisione

surfboard la tavola da surf

swallow v ingoiare

sweater il maglione

sweatshirt la felpa

sweet (taste) dolce; **~s [BE]** le caramelle

swelling il gonfiore

swim v nuotare; **~suit** il costume da bagno

symbol (keyboard) il simbolo

synagogue la sinagoga

T

table il tavolo

tablet (medicine) la compressa

take v prendere; **~**

away [BE] portare via

tampon il tampone

taste v assaggiare

taxi il taxi

team la squadra

teaspoon il cucchiaino

telephone il telefono

temple (religious) il tempio

temporary provvisorio

tennis il tennis

tent la tenda; **~ peg** il picchetto da tenda; **~ pole** il paletto da tenda

terminal (airport) il terminal

terracotta la terracotta

terrible terribile

text v **(send a message)** inviare SMS; **~** n **(message)** il testo

thank v ringraziare; **~ you** grazie

that che

theater il teatro

theft il furto

there là

thief il ladro

thirsty assetato

this questo

throat la gola

ticket il biglietto; **~ office** la biglietteria; **~ed passenger** il passeggero con biglietto

tie (clothing) la cravatta

time il tempo; **~table [BE]** l'orario

tire lo pneumatico

tired stanco

tissue il fazzoletto di carta

tobacconist il tabaccaio

today oggi

toe il dito del piede; **~nail** l'unghia

toilet [BE] la toilette; **~ paper** la carta igienica

tomorrow domani

tongue la lingua

tonight stanotte

too troppo

tooth il dente; **~paste** il dentifricio

total (amount) il totale

tough (food) duro

tourist il turista; **~ information office** l'ufficio informazioni turistiche

tour la gita

tow truck il carro attrezzi

towel l'asciugamano

tower la torre

town la città; **~ hall** il municipio; **~ map** la cartina della città; **~ square** la piazza della città

toy il giocattolo; **~ store** il negozio di giocattoli

track (train) il binario

traditional tradizionale

traffic light il semaforo

trail il sentiero; **~ map** la mappa dei sentieri

trailer la roulotte

train il treno; **~ station** la stazione ferroviaria

transfer v **(change trains/flights)** cambiare; **~ (money)** trasferire

translate v tradurre

trash la spazzatura

travel viaggiare; **~ agency** l'agenzia viaggi; **~ sickness (air)** il mal d'aria; **~ sickness (car)** il mal d'auto; **~ sickness (sea)** il mal di mare; **~ers**

tree l'albero

trim (hair) una spuntatina

trip il viaggio

trolley [BE] il carrello

trousers i pantaloni

T-shirt la maglietta

turn off v spegnere

turn on v accendere

TV la TV

type v battere a macchina

tyre [BE] lo pneumatico

U

United Kingdom (U.K.) il Regno Unito

United States (U.S.) gli Stati Uniti

ugly brutto

umbrella l'ombrello

unattended incustodito

unconscious inconscio

underground [BE] la metropolitana; **~ station [BE]** la stazione della metropolitana

underpants le mutande

understand v capire

underwear la biancheria intima

university l'università

unleaded (gas) senza piombo

upper superiore

upset stomach lo stomaco in disordine

urgent urgente

use v usare

username il nome utente

V

vacancy la disponibilità

vacation la vacanza

vaccination la vaccinazione

vacuum cleaner l'aspirapolvere

vaginal infection l'infezione vaginale

valid valido

valley la valle

valuable di valore

value il valore

VAT [BE] l'IVA

vegetarian vegetariano

vehicle registration il numero di targa

viewpoint la prospettiva

village il villaggio

vineyard il vigneto

visa il visto

visit v visitare; **~ing hours** gli orari di visita

visually impaired ipovedente

volleyball game la partita di pallavolo

vomit v vomitare

W

wait v attendere; **~** n l'attesa; **~ing room** la sala d'attesa

waiter il cameriere

waitress la cameriera

wake v svegliare, svegliarsi; **~-up call** il servizio sveglia

walk v camminare; **~** n la passeggiata; **~ing route** il percorso pedonale

wallet il portafogli

warm v **(something)** riscaldare; **~** adj **(temperature)** caldo

washing machine la lavatrice

watch l'orologio

water skis lo sci d'acqua

waterfall la cascata

weather il tempo

week la settimana;
~end il fine setti-
mana; ~ly
settimanalmente
welcome v accogliere
west ovest
what (question) cosa
wheelchair la sedia a
rotelle; ~ ramp la
rampa per sedia a
rotelle
when (question)
quando
where (question)

dove
white bianco; ~ gold
l'oro bianco
who (question) chi
widowed vedovo
wife la moglie
window la finestra; ~
case la vetrina
windsurfer il windsurf
wine list la carta
dei vini
wireless wireless; ~
internet l'Internet
wireless; ~ internet

service il servizio
Internet wireless; ~
phone il telefono
cordless
with con
withdraw v
ritirare; ~al (bank)
il prelievo
without senza
woman la donna
wool la lana
work v lavorare
wrap v incartare
wrist il polso

write v scrivere

Y

year l'anno
yellow giallo; ~ gold
l'oro giallo
yes sì
yesterday ieri
young giovane
youth hostel l'ostello
della gioventù

Z

zoo lo zoo

ITALIAN–ENGLISH

A

a buon mercato
inexpensive
a destra right
(direction)
a girocollo crew neck
a notte per night
a settimana per week
a sinistra left
(direction)
a tempo pieno
full-time
l'abbazia abbey
l'abbigliamento
clothing
abbracciare to hug
l'abito suit
accendere v light
(cigarette); ~ v turn
on (lights)
l'accendino lighter
accessibile ai disabili
handicapped- [disa-

bled BE] accessible
l'accesso access
accettare v accept
accogliere v welcome
l'acconciatura
hairstyle
l'acconto cash
advance
l'acqua water; ~ calda
hot water; ~ potabile
drinking water;
~scooter jet ski
l'adattatore adapter
addebitare v charge
(credit card)
l'aereo airplane
l'aeroporto airport
affamato hungry
affittare v rent
[hire BE]
l'agenzia agency; ~
viaggi travel agency
l'aggressione attack

(on person)
l'agopuntura acu-
puncture
l'AIDS AIDS
aiutare to help
l'aiuto n help
al giorno per day
l'albero tree
all'angolo on the
corner
allattare breastfeed
allergico allergic
l'alloggio accom-
modation
all'ora per hour
alto high
amare v love (someone)
l'ambulanza am-
bulance
americano American
l'amico friend
l'amore n love
analcolico non-

alcoholic
andare v go (some-
where); ~ bene fit
(clothing)
l'andata e ritorno
round-trip
l'anello ring
anemico anemic
l'anestesia anesthesia
l'animale animal
l'anno year
annullare v cancel
l'antibiotico antibiotic
l'antipasto appetizer
[starter BE]
l'anziano senior citizen
aperto adj open
l'appartamento apart-
ment
l'appendice appendix
(body part)
l'appuntamento
appointment

appuntito sharp

l'apribottiglie bottle opener

aprire v open

l'apriscatole can opener

arancione orange (color)

l'argento silver; **~ massiccio** sterling silver

l'aria condizionata air conditioning

l'armadietto locker; **~ dei bagagli** luggage locker

l'aromaterapia aromatherapy

arrivare v arrive

arrivederla goodbye

gli arrivi arrivals (airport)

l'arte art

l'arteria artery

gli articoli casalinghi household goods

l'artrite arthritis

l'ascensore elevator

l'asciugacapelli hair dryer

l'asciugamano towel

asmatico asthmatic

l'aspirapolvere vacuum cleaner

l'aspirina aspirin

assaggiare v taste

l'assegno n check (payment) [cheque BE]

assetato thirsty

l'assicurazione insurance

l'assorbente sanitary

napkin [pad BE]

l'astuccio della macchina fotografica camera case

attendere v wait

l'attesa n wait

attraente attractive

l'attrattiva attraction (place); **~ principale** main attraction

l'attrezzatura equipment; **~ da immersione** snorkeling equipment; **~ subacquea** diving equipment

gli auricolari headphones

Australia Australia

australiano Australian

l'auto car; **~bus** bus; **~ con il cambio automatico** automatic car; **~ con il cambio manuale** manual car; **~ a noleggio** rental [hire BE] car

automatico automatic

l'autonoleggio car rental [hire BE]

l'autostrada highway [motorway BE]

avere v have; **~ la nausea** v be nauseous

avvertire v notify

l'avvocato lawyer

B

la babysitter babysitter

baciare v kiss

il bagaglio luggage

[baggage BE]; **~ a mano** carry-on [hand luggage BE]

il bagnino lifeguard

il bagno bathroom

ballare v dance

il ballo dancing

il balsamo conditioner

il bambino child

la bambola doll

la banca bank

il bancomat ATM, ATM card, debit card

la banconota n bill (money) [note BE]

il bar bar; **~ per gay** gay bar

il barbecue barbecue

il barbiere barber

la barca boat; **~ a remi** rowboat

il baseball baseball

il basketball basketball

basso low

i bastoncini cinesi chopsticks

battere a macchina v type

la batteria battery

il bebè baby

beige beige

bello beautiful

il belvedere overlook (scenic place)

ben riposato well-rested

la benda bandage

bene good

la benzina gas (vehicle) [petrol BE]

il benzinaio gas

[petrol BE] station

bere v drink

la bevanda n drink

la biancheria intima underwear

bianco white

il biberon baby bottle

la biblioteca library

il bicchiere glass (drinking)

la bicicletta bicycle

la biglietteria ticket office

il biglietto ticket; **~ del bus** bus ticket; **~ elettronico** e-ticket; **~ da visita** business card

il bikini bikini

il binario platform; track (train)

blu blue

la bocca mouth

la borsa bag

la borsetta purse [handbag BE]

il bosco forest

la bottiglia bottle

il box playpen

il braccialetto bracelet

il braccio arm

bruciare v burn

brutto ugly

la buca delle lettere postbox

buongiorno good morning

buon pomeriggio good afternoon

buonasera good evening

buono *adj* good
il bus espresso express bus
la busta envelope

C

il cabaret cabaret
la cabina cabin
il caffè cafe, coffee
il calcio soccer
caldo hot (temperature)
il calore heat (heating BE)
le calorie calories
il calzino sock
cambiare *v* change; ~ *v* exchange; ~ *v* transfer
il cambio *n* change (money); ~ *n* exchange (place); ~ **valuta** currency exchange
la cameriera waitress
il cameriere waiter
la camicetta blouse
la camicia shirt
camminare *v* walk
campeggiare *v* camp
il campeggio campsite
il campione specimen
il campo field (sports); ~ **da golf** golf course; ~ **di battaglia** battleground
il Canada Canada
canadese Canadian
il canalone canyon
cancellare *v* clear (on an ATM)

il cane da guida guide dog
i capelli hair
capire *v* understand
il cappello hat
il cappotto coat
la caraffa carafe
le caramelle candy [sweet BE]
il carbone charcoal
carino cute
caro expensive
il carrello cart [trolley BE]; ~ **bagagli** luggage cart
il carro attrezzi tow truck
la carta card, paper; ~ **di credito** credit card; ~ **da cucina** paper towel; ~ **igienica** toilet paper; ~ **d'imbarco** boarding pass; ~ **stagnola** aluminum [kitchen BE] foil; ~ **dei vini** wine list
la cartina map; ~ **della città** town map; ~ **delle piste** trail [piste BE] map; ~ **stradale** road map
la cartolina postcard
il cartone carton
la casa house
la cascata waterfall
il casco helmet
il casinò casino
la cassa case (container); ~**forte** safe (for valuables)

la cassetta della posta mailbox
il cassiere cashier
il castello castle
la cattedrale cathedral
il cavatappi corkscrew
la caviglia ankle
il CD CD
Celsius Celsius
la cena dinner
il centimetro centimeter
il centro downtown area; ~ **business** business center; ~ **commerciale** shopping mall [centre BE]
la ceramica pottery
la ceretta wax; ~ **all'inguine** bikini wax; ~ **per sopracciglie** eyebrow wax
il certificato certificate
il cestino basket (grocery store)
che that
il check-in check-in (hotel/airport)
chi who
chiamare *v* call
la chiamata *n* call
la chiave key; ~ **elettronica** key card; ~ **della stanza** room key
la chiesa church
il chilo kilo; ~**grammo** kilogram; ~**metraggio** mileage;

~**metro** kilometer; ~**metro quadrato** square kilometer
chiudere *v* close (a shop); ~ *v* lock
chiuso closed
le ciabatte slippers
ciao hi, bye
il cibo food
il ciclismo cycling
il ciclo period (menstrual)
il cinema movie theater
cinese Chinese
la cintura belt
il circuito racetrack
la città town
il ciuccio pacifier [soother BE]
la classe class; ~ **business** business class; ~ **economica** economy class
il club club; ~ **di ballo** dance club; ~ **jazz** jazz club; ~ **per gay** gay club
il codice code; ~ **di abbigliamento** dress code; ~ **PIN** personal identification number (PIN)
la coincidenza connection (flight)
la colazione breakfast
la collana necklace
il collant pantyhose
il collega colleague
il collegamento connection (internet); ~ **wireless a Internet** wireless internet

collegarsi v connect (internet)
la collina hill
il collo neck
la colonia cologne
il colore color
il coltello knife
come how
il commissariato police station
la compagnia aerea airline
la compagnia di assi-curazione insurance company
compilare v fill out (form)
il compleanno birthday
comporre il numero v dial
comprare v buy
la compressa tablet (medicine)
il computer computer
con with
il concerto concert
la condizione condition (medical)
la conferenza conference
confermare v confirm
la congestione congestion
il consolato consulate
il consulente consultant
contagioso contagious
i contanti n cash
contattare to contact
il conto n bill (of sale); ~ account; ~

corrente checking [current BE] account
il contorno side dish
controllare v check (luggage)
il controllo passaporti passport control
convalidare v stamp (a ticket)
la coperta blanket
il coperto cover charge
la coppa bowl
il corridoio aisle
corto short
cosa what (question)
la coscia thigh
costare v cost
costipato constipated
il costo charge (cost)
la costola rib (body part)
il costume da bagno swimsuit
il cotone cotton
il crampo mestruale menstrual cramp
la cravatta tie (clothing)
la crema cream (ointment); ~ **antisettica** antiseptic cream; ~ **da barba** shaving cream
il cristallo crystal
la cuccetta berth
il cucchiaino teaspoon
il cucchiaio spoon
la cucina kitchen, stove
cucinare v cook
la culla crib

il cuore heart
il cuscino pillow

D

da banco over the counter (medication)
danneggiare v damage
danneggiato damaged
dare v give; ~ **da mangiare** v feed
la data date (calendar)
del pomeriggio p.m.
il denaro money
il dente tooth
la dentiera denture
il dentifricio toothpaste
il dentista dentist
il deodorante deodorant
depositare v deposit
il deposito n deposit
derubato robbed
il deserto desert
il detersivo detergent; ~ **per i piatti** dishwashing liquid
di fronte a opposite
di valore valuable
diabetico diabetic
il diamante diamond
la diarrea diarrhea
dichiarare v declare
il diesel diesel
dietro around (the corner), behind (direction)
difficile difficult
digitale digital
la direzione direction
il disabile handi-capped [disabled BE]

la disponibilità vacancy
il disturbo cardiaco heart condition
il dito finger; ~ **del piede** toe
divorziare v divorce
la doccia shower
la dogana customs
dolce sweet (taste)
il dollaro dollar (U.S.)
il dolore hurt (pain); ~ **al petto** chest pain
la domanda question
domani tomorrow
domestico domestic
la donna woman
dopo after; ~**barba** aftershave
doppiato dubbed
dormire v sleep
il dormitorio dormitory
dove where (question)
la dozzina dozen
dritto straight
durante during
duro tough (food)
duty-free duty-free
il DVD DVD

E

e and
l'eccesso excess; ~ **di velocità** speeding
economico cheap
l'edicola newsstand
l'edificio building; ~ **del parlamento** parliament building
l'effetto collaterale side effect

eliminare v delete (computer)

l'e-mail n e-mail

l'emergenza emergency

l'enoteca liquor store [off-licence BE]

entrare v enter

l'entrata entrance

l'erboristeria health food store

l'errore mistake

esausto exhausted

l'escursione excursion; **~ in pullman** bus tour

esperto expert

espresso express

essere v be

est east

estrarre v extract (tooth)

l'età age

l'euro euro

extra extra; **~ large** extra large

F

facile easy

la famiglia family

fare v do; **~ l'autostop** v hitchhike; **~ la ceretta** v wax; **~ un incidente** v crash (car); **~ il logoff** v log off (computer); **~ il logon** v log on (computer); **~ lo shopping** v shop; **le valigie** v pack

la farmacia pharmacy

[chemist BE]

il fast food fast food

la fattoria farm

la fattura bill [invoice BE]

fatturare v bill (charge)

il fax n fax

il fazzoletto di carta tissue

la febbre fever

il fegato liver (body part)

felice happy

la felpa sweatshirt

fenomenale stunning

fermarsi v stop

la fermata n stop; **~ del bus** bus stop

il ferro da stiro n iron (clothes)

la fetta slice (of something)

il fiammifero n match (wooden stick)

il film movie

il filtro solare sunblock, sunscreen

il fine settimana weekend

la finestra window

finire v end

il fiore flower

firmare v sign

il fiume river

la fontana fountain

le forbici scissors

la forchetta fork

la foresta pluviale rainforest

il fornello da campeggio camping stove

la fortezza fort

la foto photo; **~ digitale** digital photo; **~copia** photocopy; **~grafia** photography

il francobollo n stamp (postage)

il fratello brother

freddo cold (temperature)

il freezer freezer

i freni brakes (car)

frequentare to attend

fresco cool (temperature); **~** fresh

la fretta rush

il frigorifero refrigerator

la frutta e verdura produce

il fruttivendolo grocery store

fumare v smoke

la funivia cable car

il fuoco fire

fuori outside

il furto theft; **~ con scasso** break-in (burglary)

G

la gamba leg

la gara di golf golf tournament

il garage garage

il gas gas (heating); **~ per cucina** cooking gas

la gastronomia delicatessen

gay gay

il gel gel (hair)

gelato icy

il ghiaccio ice

la giacca jacket

giallo yellow

il giardino botanico botanical garden

il ginecologo gynecologist

il ginocchio knee

giocare v play

il giocattolo toy

la gioielleria jewelry

il gioielliere jeweler

il giornale newspaper

il giorno day

giovane young

la gita tour; **~ turistica** sightseeing tour

il giubbotto di salvataggio life jacket

la giuntura joint (body part)

la goccia drop (medicine)

godersi v enjoy

la gola throat

il gomito elbow

la gomma rubber; **~ a terra** flat tire; **~ da masticare** chewing gum

il gonfiore swelling

la gonna skirt

i gradi degrees (temperature)

il grammo gram

grande big, large; **~ magazzino** department store

grazie thank you

grigio gray

la grotta cave
il gruppo group
guardare v look
il guasto breakdown
la guida guide, guide book
guidare v drive

H

l'hockey hockey;
~ **su ghiaccio** ice hockey
l'hotel hotel

I

l'ibuprofene ibuprofen
l'identificazione identification
ieri yesterday
imbarcarsi v board
l'impermeabile raincoat
in in; ~ **pensione** retired
incartare v wrap
incassare v cash
l'incidente accident
incidere v engrave
incinta pregnant
includere v include
inconscio unconscious
incontrare v meet (someone)
l'incontro di boxe boxing match
l'incrocio intersection
incustodito unattended
l'indirizzo address;
~ **e-mail** e-mail address
infastidire v bother

l'infermiere nurse
infetto infected
l'infezione vaginale vaginal infection
le informazioni information (phone)
inglese English
ingoiare v swallow
l'ingresso admission
iniziare v begin, start
inserire v insert
l'insetto bug
insipido bland
l'insolazione sunstroke
l'insonnia insomnia
l'insulina insulin
interessante interesting
intermedio intermediate
internazionale international (airport area)
l'Internet internet; ~ **caffè** internet cafe; ~ **wireless** wireless internet
l'interno extension (phone)
l'interprete interpreter
l'intestino intestine
intollerante al lattosio lactose intolerant
l'intrattenimento entertainment
inviare v send, ship (mail); ~ **e-mail** v e-mail; ~ **per fax** v fax; ~ **SMS** v text (send a message)

ipermetrope far-[long- BE] sighted
ipovedente visually impaired
l'ippodromo horsetrack
l'Irlanda Ireland
irlandese Irish
l'irritazione rash
l'Italia Italy
italiano Italian
l'IVA sales tax [VAT BE]

J

il jazz jazz
i jeans jeans

L

là there
la casa prefabbricata mobile home
la stanza singola single room
il labbro lip
la lacca hairspray
il ladro thief
il lago lake
la lametta razor blade; ~ **usa e getta** disposable razor
la lampadina lightbulb
la lana wool
il latte in polvere formula (baby)
il lato side
la lavanderia laundry; ~ **a gettone** laundromat [launderette BE]
il lavandino sink
il lavasecco dry

cleaner
la lavastoviglie dishwasher
la lavatrice washing machine
lavorare v work
il lavoro business
lentamente slowly
la lente lens; ~ **a contatto** contact lens
il lenzuolo sheet
la lettera letter
il lettino cot
il letto bed; ~ **matrimoniale** double bed; ~ **a una piazza** single bed
la lezione lesson
libero available, free
la libreria bookstore
il libro book
il lift pass lift pass
la lima nail file
la linea line (train)
la lingua tongue
il lino linen
il litro liter
locale local
lontano far
la lozione lotion
la luce light (overhead)
il lunapark amusement park
lungo long

M

la macchina fotografica camera; ~ **digitale** digital camera

il macellaio butcher
la madre mother
la maglietta T-shirt
il maglione sweater
magnifico magnificent
il mal sickness; **~ d'aria** motion sickness (air); **~ d'auto** motion sickness (car); **~ di gola** sore throat; **~ di mare** motion sickness (sea); **~ d'orecchio** earache; **~ di schiena** backache; **~ di stomaco** stomachache; **~ di testa** headache
malato sick [ill BE]
malattia sessualmente trasmissibile sexually transmitted disease (STD)
mancante missing
mangiare v eat
le maniche sleeves; **~ corte** short sleeves; **~ lunghe** long sleeves
il manicure manicure
la mano hand
il mare sea
il marito husband
marrone brown
il martello hammer
la mascella jaw
il massaggio massage; **~ sportivo** sports massage
il mattino morning

del mattino a.m.
il meccanico mechanic
la medicina medicine
il medico doctor
medio medium (size)
meno less
il menù menu; **~ delle bevande** drink menu; **~ per bambini** children's menu
il mercato market
le merci goods
il mese month
la messa mass (church service)
il messaggio message; **~ istantaneo** instant message
la metà half
il metro quadrato square meter
la metropolitana subway [underground BE]
la mezz'ora half hour
la mezzanotte midnight
il mezzo chilo half-kilo
mezzogiorno noon [midday BE]
il microonde microwave
migliore better
il migliore best
il minibar mini-bar
il minuto minute
miope near- [short-BE] sighted

misurare v measure (someone, something)
il misurino measuring spoon
mobile mobile
la mobilità mobility
i mocassini loafers
il mocio mop
modificare v alter (clothing)
il modulo form (fill-in)
la moglie wife
la moneta coin
la montagna mountain
il monumento memorial (place)
la moschea mosque
mostrare v show
la motocicletta motorcycle
il motore motor
il motoscafo motor boat
la mountain bike mountain bike
la mousse mousse (hair)
la multa fine (fee for breaking law)
il municipio town hall
il muscolo muscle
il museo museum
la musica music; **~ classica** classical music; **~ folk** folk music; **~ pop** pop music
le mutande underpants

N

il naso nose
il nastro trasportatore conveyor belt
le natiche buttocks
la nazionalità nationality
necessitare v need
il negozio store; **~ d'abbigliamento** clothing store; **~ d'antiquariato** antique store; **~ di articoli da regalo** gift shop; **~ di articoli sportivi** sporting goods store; **~ di calzature** shoe store; **~ di fotografia** camera store; **~ di giocattoli** toy store; **~ di musica** music store; **~ di souvenir** souvenir store
nero black
la neve snow
nevoso snowy
niente nothing
il nightclub nightclub
il nipote grandchild
no no
noioso boring
il nome name; **~ utente** username
non fumatori non-smoking
il nonno grandparent
nord north
normale regular
la notte night

il numero number; **~ di fax** fax number; **~ di patente** driver's license number; **~ di targa** vehicle registration; **~ di telefono** phone number
nuotare v swim

O

gli occhiali glasses; **~ da sole** sunglasses
l'occhio eye
oggi today
OK OK
l'olio oil
l'ombrello umbrella
l'opera opera
ora now
l'ora hour
gli orari di visita visiting hours
l'orario schedule [timetable BE]; **~ d'apertura** business hours; **~ d'ufficio** office hours
l'orchestra orchestra
ordinare v order
gli orecchini earrings
l'orecchio ear
l'oro gold; **~bianco** white gold; **~ giallo** yellow gold
l'orologio watch; **~ da parete** wall clock
l'ospedale hospital
l'osso bone
l'ostello hostel; **~**

della gioventù youth hostel
l'ottico optician
l'otturazione filling (tooth)
ovest west

P

il pacchetto package
la padella frying pan
il padre father
il pagamento del conto check-out (hotel)
pagare v pay
il palazzo palace
la palestra gym
il paletto da tenda tent pole
la panetteria bakery
il pannolino diaper [nappy BE]
i pantaloncini corti shorts
i pantaloni pants [trousers BE]
il paracetamolo acetaminophen [paracetamol BE]
parcheggiare v park
il parcheggio parking garage; **~** parking lot [car park BE]
il parco n park; **~ giochi** playground
parlare v speak
il parrucchiere hair salon
le partenze departures (airport)
partire v leave
la partita game,

match; **~ di football** soccer [football game BE]; **~ di pallavolo** volleyball game
part-time part-time
il passaggio lift
il passaporto passport
passare v pass through
il passeggero passenger; **~ con biglietto** ticketed passenger
la passeggiata n walk
il passeggino stroller [pushchair BE]
la password password
la pasticceria pastry shop
il pasto meal
il pediatra pediatrician
il pedicure pedicure
il pedone pedestrian
la pelle leather, skin
la pellicola per alimenti plastic wrap [cling film BE]
il peltro pewter
il pene penis
la penicillina penicillin
la penna pen
la pensione bed and breakfast
la pentola saucepan, pot
per for, per; **~ favore** please; **~ fumatori** smoking (area); **~ la notte** overnight
il percorso route; **~ alternativo** alternate route;

~ ciclabile bike route; **~ pedonale** walking route
perdere v lose (something)
la perdita discharge (bodily fluid)
pericoloso dangerous
il periodo period (of time)
la perla pearl
permettere v allow, permit
perso lost
il pettine comb
il petto chest (body part)
il petto breast
il pezzo piece
piacere v like
il piacere pleasure
il piano floor [storey BE]
il pianterreno ground floor
la piantina del negozio store directory
il piatto plate; **~ principale** main course
la piazza della città town square
piccante hot (spicy)
il picchetto da tenda tent peg
piccolo little, petite, small
il piede foot
il pigiama pajamas
la pillola Pill (birth control)

la pioggia rain

piovoso rainy

la piscina pool; ~ **per bambini** kiddie [paddling BE] pool; ~ **esterna** outdoor pool; ~ **interna** indoor pool

pista piste [BE]

più more; ~ **basso** lower; ~ **economico** cheaper; ~ **forte** louder; ~ **grande** bigger; ~ **lento** slower; ~ **piccolo** smaller; ~ **tardi** later; ~ **veloce** faster

la pizzeria pizzeria

il pizzo lace

il platino platinum

lo pneumatico tire [tyre BE]

la polizia police

il polmone lung

il polso wrist

il pomeriggio afternoon

la pompa dell'aria air pump

il ponte bridge

la porta door; ~ **antincendio** fire door

il portachiavi key ring

il portafogli wallet

portare v bring; ~ **indietro** v return (something); ~ **via** to go [take away BE]

la porzione portion; ~ **per bambini** children's portion

la posa exposure (film)

la posta n mail [post BE]; ~ **aerea** airmail

il posto seat; ~ **sul corridoio** aisle seat

il pranzo lunch

la precedenza right of way

il prefisso area code; ~ **del paese** country code

il prelievo withdrawal (bank)

prendere v take

prenotare v reserve

la prenotazione reservation

la presa elettrica electric outlet

prescrivere v prescribe

presentare v introduce

il preservativo condom

la pressione sanguigna blood pressure

presto early

la previsione forecast

il prezzo price

prima before, earlier; ~ **classe** first class

primo first

il principiante beginner, novice

il problema problem

i prodotti per la pulizia cleaning supplies

profondamente deeply

il profumo perfume

il programma n

schedule

programmare v schedule

proibire v prohibit

pronto ready

pronunciare v pronounce

la prospettiva viewpoint

prossimo next

provvisorio temporary

pubblico public

pulire v clean

pulito adj clean

la pulizia del viso facial

la puntura sting; ~ **d'insetto** insect bite

Q

quadrato square

qualche some

la qualità quality

qualsiasi cosa anything

quando when (question)

quanto how much (question)

questo this

qui here

R

la racchetta racket (sports)

le racchette poles (skiing)

raccogliere v pick up (something)

raccomandare v recommend

la raccomandata

registered mail

la raccomandazione recommendation

il radiatore heater

il raffreddore cold (sickness)

la ragazza girl, girlfriend

il ragazzo boy, boyfriend

raggiungere v reach (get hold of)

il rame copper

la rampa per sedia a rotelle wheelchair ramp

il rap rap (music)

la reazione allergica allergic reaction

la reception reception

il reclamo complaint

il regalo gift

il reggiseno bra

la regione region

il Regno Unito United Kingdom (U.K.)

la relazione relationship

il rene kidney (body part)

il repellente per gli insetti insect repellent

il residente UE EU resident

respirare v breathe

il ricambio part (for car)

il riciclaggio n recycling

la ricetta prescription

ricevere v receive

la **ricevuta** receipt

il **riciclaggio** *n* recycling

riempire *v* fill

rifiutare *v* decline (credit card)

ringraziare *v* thank

riparare *v* fix, mend, repair

ripetere *v* repeat

ripido steep

il **responsabile** manager

il **riscaldamento** heating

riscaldare *v* warm (something)

la **riserva naturale** nature preserve

i **risparmi** savings (account)

il **ristorante** restaurant

ritardare *v* delay

ritirare *v* withdraw

il **ritiro bagagli** baggage claim

la **riunione** meeting

la **rivista** magazine

romantico romantic

rompere *v* break

rosa pink

rosso red

rotto broken

la **roulotte** trailer

le **rovine** ruins

rubare *v* rob, steal

rubato stolen

il **rugby** rugby

il **rullino** film (camera)

il **ruscello** stream

S

il **sacchetto per i rifiuti** garbage [rubbish BE] bag

il **sacco a pelo** sleeping bag

la **sala** room; **~ congressi** convention hall; **~ d'attesa** waiting room; **~ da concerti** concert hall; **~ da pranzo** dining room; **~ giochi** arcade; **~ riunioni** meeting room

il **salone di bellezza** nail salon

la **salute** health

Salute! Cheers!

salvare *v* save (computer)

salve hello

la **salvietta per neonati** baby wipe

i **sandali** sandals

il **sangue** blood

sanguinare *v* bleed

il **santuario** shrine

il **sapone** soap

la **sauna** sauna

la **sbornia** hangover

le **scale** stairs; **~ mobili** escalators

lo **scanner** scanner

le **scarpe** shoes; **~ da neve** snowshoes; **~ basse** flat shoes; **~ col tacco alto** high-heeled shoes; **~ da ginnastica** sneakers

gli **scarponi da**

la **montagna** hiking boots

la **scatola** box

lo **scatolame** canned good

scendere *v* get off (a train, bus, subway)

la **scheda** card; **~ memoria** memory card; **~ telefonica** phone card

lo **schermo** display

la **schiena** back (body part)

lo **sci** *n* ski; **~ d'acqua** water skis

sciare *v* ski

la **sciarpa** scarf

la **scienza** science

scippare *v* mug

la **scogliera** cliff

la **scolapasta** colander

scollegare *v* disconnect (computer)

lo **scollo a V** V-neck

scommettere *v* place a bet

scomparso missing

lo **sconto** discount

lo **scontrino bagagli** luggage [baggage BE] ticket

lo **scooter** moped

la **scopa** broom

la **scottatura** sunburn

scrivere *v* spell, write

la **scuola** school

scuro dark

scusare *v* excuse

scusi sorry (apology)

sedersi *v* sit

la **sedia** chair; **~ a rotelle** wheelchair; **~ a sdraio** deck chair

il **sedile per bambino** child's seat

il **seggiolino per auto** car seat

il **seggiolone** highchair

la **seggiovia** chair lift

il **self-service** self-service

il **semaforo** traffic light

il **seminario** seminar

il **senso unico** one-way street

il **sentiero** path, trail

senza without; **~ grassi** fat free; **~ piombo** unleaded (gas)

separato separated (marriage)

la **sera** evening

serio serious

la **serratura** *n* lock

i **servizi di pulizia domestica** housekeeping services

il **servizio** service (in a restaurant); **~ completo** full-service; **~ di lavanderia** laundry service; **~ in camera** room service; **~ Internet** internet service; **~ Internet wireless** wireless internet service; **~ sveglia** wake-up call

la seta silk
la settimana week
settimanalmente weekly
lo shampoo shampoo
lo shopping shopping
sì yes
la sicurezza security
sicuro safe (protected)
la sigaretta cigarette
il sigaro cigar
il simbolo symbol (keyboard)
la sinagoga synagogue
single single (marriage)
lo ski lift drag lift, ski lift
lo slip briefs (clothing)
lo smalto enamel (jewelry)
lo snack bar snack bar
lo snowboard snowboard
il sole sun
soleggiato sunny
solo alone, only; **~ andata** one-way (ticket)
la soluzione per lenti a contatto contact lens solution
la sonnolenza drowsiness
sopra over
sordo deaf
la sorella sister
il sottotitolo subtitle
il souvenir souvenir
la spalla shoulder
la spatola spatula
la spazzatura trash

[rubbish BE]
la spazzola hairbrush
lo specialista specialist (doctor)
la specialità special (food)
spedire v mail
spegnere v turn off (lights)
lo spettacolo n play (theater); **~ di danza** ballet
la spiaggia beach
la spilla brooch
la spina dorsale spine (body part)
spingere v push (door sign)
lo spogliatoio fitting room
sporco dirty
lo sport sport
sposare v marry
sposato married
la spuntatina trim (hair)
la squadra team
squisito delicious
lo stadio stadium
lo stagno pond
stampare v print
la stampa n print; **~ digitale** digital print; **~ singola** single print
stanco tired
stanotte tonight
la stanza room
stare v stay
gli Stati Uniti United States (U.S.)
la station wagon

station wagon [estate car BE]
la statua statue
la stazione station; **~ degli autobus** bus station; **~ dei bus** bus station; **~ ferroviaria** train station [railway station BE]; **~ della metropolitana** subway station [underground station BE]; **~ di servizio** gas station [petrol station BE]; **~ termale** spa
la stecca di sigarette carton of cigarettes
le sterline pounds (British sterling)
stesso same
stirare v iron, press (clothing)
gli stivali boots
lo stomaco stomach; **~ in disordine** upset stomach
stordito dizzy
la storta sprain
strano strange
straordinario amazing
lo studente student
studiare v study
stuprare v rape
lo stupro n rape
lo sturalavandini plunger
sud south
la super super (fuel)
superiore upper
il supermercato supermarket
la supervisione

supervision
svegliare, svegliarsi v wake
sviluppare v develop (film)
svuotare v empty

T
il tabaccaio tobacconist
la taglia size; **~ forte** plus size
tagliare v cut (hair)
il taglio n cut (injury), haircut
il tampone tampon
tardi late (time)
la tariffa fee
la tasca pocket
la tassa duty (tax)
il tasso di cambio exchange rate
la tavola da surf surfboard
il tavolo table
il taxi taxi
la tazza cup; **~ di misurazione** measuring cup
il teatro theater; **~ dell'opera** opera house
telefonare v phone
la telefonata phone call
il telefonino cell [mobile BE] phone
il telefono n phone; **~ telephone**; **~ cordless** wireless phone; **~ pubblico** pay phone

il telone impermeabile groundcloth [groundsheet BE]

il tempio temple (religious)

il tempo time, weather

la tenda tent

il tennis tennis

la terapia ad ossigeno oxygen treatment

le terme hot spring

il terminal terminal (airport)

la terracotta terracotta

terribile terrible

la tessera card; ~ associativa membership card; ~ dell'assicurazione insurance card; ~ internazionale dello studente international student card

la testa head (body part)

il testo n text (message)

tirare v pull (door sign)

la toilette restroom [toilet BE]

la torcia elettrica flashlight

la torre tower

la tosse n cough

tossire v cough

il totale total (amount)

il tovagliolo napkin

tradizionale traditional

tradurre v translate

il traghetto ferry

tranquillo quiet

trasferire v transfer (money)

il travellers cheque travelers check [travelers cheque BE]

il treno train; ~ espresso express train

triste sad

troppo too

tuffarsi v dive

il turista tourist

la TV TV

U

l'uccello bird

l'ufficio office; ~ di cambio currency exchange office; ~ informazioni information desk; ~ informazioni turistiche tourist information office; ~ oggetti smarriti lost and found; ~ postale post office; ~ prenotazioni reservation desk

ultimo last

una volta once

l'unghia fingernail, toenail

unire v join

l'università university

uno one

l'uomo man

urgente urgent

usa e getta disposable

usare v use

uscire v exit

l'uscita gate (airport), exit; ~ d'emergenza emergency exit

l'utensile utensil

V

la vacanza vacation [holiday BE]

la vaccinazione vaccination

la vagina vagina

il vagone letto sleeper [sleeping BE] car

valido valid

la valigia suitcase

la valle valley

il valore value

la valuta currency

il vaso jar

vecchio old

vedere v see

vedovo widowed

vegetariano vegetarian

il veleno poison

veloce fast

vendere v sell

venire v come

il ventaglio fan (souvenir)

il ventilatore fan (appliance)

il verbale di polizia police report

verde green

vero real

la vescica bladder

il vestito dress (piece of clothing)

la vetrina window

case

la vetrinetta display case

il vetro glass (material)

la vetta peak (of a mountain)

il viaggio trip

vicino close, near, nearby, next to

i vigili del fuoco fire department

il vigneto vineyard

il villaggio village

viola purple

la visita turistica sightseeing

visitare v visit

il viso face

il visto visa

la vita life

la vitamina vitamin

vivere v live

il volo flight; ~ internazionale international flight; ~ nazionale domestic flight

vomitare v vomit

W

il WC da campeggio chemical toilet

il windsurf windsurfer

Z

lo zaino backpack

la zona area; ~ commerciale shopping area; ~ picnic picnic area

lo zoo zoo

INDEX

pocket guide

VENICE

Nineteenth Edition 2020

Editor: Zara Sekhavati
Author: Rob Ullian
Head of DTP and Pre-Press: Rebeka Davies
Managing Editor: Carine Tracanelli
Picture Editors: Tom Smyth, Aude Vauconsant
Cartography Update: Carte
Update Production: Apa Digital
Photography Credits: Alamy 4ML, 7R, 95;
Andrea Sarti/Peggy Guggenheim Collection
4BL; Anna Mockford and Nick Bonetti/Apa
Publications 34, 37, 40, 47, 70, 72, 79; Chris
Coe/Apa Publications 42, 51; Corbis 16, 31;
Danita Delimont Stock/AWL Images 24;
Dreamstime 11, 15; Hilton Hotels & resorts
7R; iStock 4TC, 5T, 5TC, 5BL, 5M, 5MC, 6L,
6R, 27, 32, 38, 43, 44, 50, 54, 57, 58, 63, 65,
74, 83, 93, 96; Marco Bottigelli/AWL Images
1; Public domain 18, 20; Ros Miller/Apa
Publications 80; Shutterstock 7L, 12, 29, 61,
76, 88, 102; Starwood Hotels & Resorts 99;
SuperStock 85
Cover Picture: AWL Images/Shutterstock

Distribution
UK, Ireland and Europe: Apa Publications
(UK) Ltd; sales@insightguides.com
United States and Canada: Ingram
Publisher Services; ips@ingramcontent.com
Australia and New Zealand: Woodslane;
info@woodslane.com.au
Southeast Asia: Apa Publications (SN) Pte;
singaporeoffice@insightguides.com

Worldwide: Apa Publications (UK) Ltd;
sales@insightguides.com

**Special Sales, Content Licensing
and CoPublishing**
Insight Guides can be purchased in bulk
quantities at discounted prices. We can
create special editions, personalised
jackets and corporate imprints. sales@
insightguides.com;
www.insightguides.biz

Contact us
Every effort has been made to provide
accurate information in this publication,
but changes are inevitable. The publisher
cannot be responsible for any resulting loss,
inconvenience or injury. We would appreciate
it if readers would call our attention to any
errors or outdated information. We also
welcome your suggestions; please contact
us at: berlitz@apaguide.co.uk
www.insightguides.com/berlitz

1 — P.le Roma - Lido S.M.E., Lido S.M.E.- P.le Roma

2 — S. Zaccaria - P.le Roma - S. Marco (Giardinetti),
S. Marco (Giardinetti) - P.le Roma - S. Zaccaria

3 — P.le Roma - Ferrovia - Murano - Ferrovia - P.le Roma

4.1 — Murano - F.te Nove - P.le Roma - F.te Nove - Murano
(Anticlockwise)

4.2 — Murano - F.te Nove - P.le Roma - F.te Nove - Murano
(Clockwise)

5.1 — Lido S.M.E.- F.te Nove - P.le Roma - S. Zaccaria - Lido S.M.E.
(Anticlockwise)

5.2 — Lido S.M.E.- S. Zaccaria - P.le Roma - F.te Nove - Lido S.M.E.
(Clockwise)

6 — P.le Roma - Lido S.M.E., Lido S.M.E.- P.le Roma

9 — Burano - Torcello, Torcello - Burano

10 — Lido S.M.E. - Zattere, Zattere - Lido S.M.E.

12 — F.te Nove - Punta Sabbioni, Punta Sabbioni - F.te Nove

13 — F.te Nove - Treporti, Treporti - F.te Nove

14 15 — Venezia - Lido S.M.E. - Punta Sabbioni,
Punta Sabbioni - Lido S.M.E. - Venezia

16 — Fusina - Venezia, Venezia - Fusina

17 — Car ferry, Tronchetto - Lido S. Nicoló - Punta Sabbior
Punta Sabbioni - Lido S. Nicoló - Tronchetto

20 — S. Zaccaria - S. Servolo - S. Lazzaro - S. Zaccaria

22 — Punta Sabbioni - Tre Archi, Tre Archi - Punta Sabbio

N — Night services

A B R — Alilaguna lines (A - Arancio, B - Blu, R -Rossa
– seasonal route)

VA — Vaporetto dell'arte

7 8 14 18 19 — Seasonal route

7 — Ticket points

Venice Vaporetti Network